hugo

ITALIAN
IN 3 MONTHS

Milena Reynolds

**YOUR ESSENTIAL GUIDE TO
UNDERSTANDING AND
SPEAKING ITALIAN**

THIRD EDITION
Series Editor Elise Bradbury
Senior Editor Amelia Petersen
Senior Art Editor Jane Ewart
Managing Editors Christine Stroyan, Carine Tracanelli
Managing Art Editor Anna Hall
Production Editor Robert Dunn
Senior Production Controller Samantha Cross
Jacket Project Art Editor Surabhi Wadhwa-Gandhi
Jacket Design Development Manager Sophia MTT
Art Director Karen Self
Associate Publishing Director Liz Wheeler
Publishing Director Jonathan Metcalf

DK INDIA
Project Art Editor Anjali Sachar
Senior DTP Designer Shanker Prasad
Managing Editor Rohan Sinha
Managing Art Editor Sudakshina Basu

This American Edition, 2022
First American Edition, 1997
Published in the United States by DK Publishing
1745 Broadway, 20th Floor, New York, NY 10019

Copyright © 1997, 2003, 2022 Dorling Kindersley Limited
DK, a Division of Penguin Random House LLC
23 24 10 9 8 7 6 5 4
004–326926–Jan/2022

Written by
Milena Reynolds
Formerly Lecturer in Italian, Morley College, London

A catalog record for this book is available from the Library of Congress.
ISBN 978-0-7440-5162-9

DK books are available at special discounts when
purchased in bulk for sales promotions, premiums,
fund-raising, or educational use.
For details, contact: DK Publishing Special Markets,
1745 Broadway, 20th Floor, New York, NY 10019
SpecialSales@dk.com

Printed and bound in China

For the curious
www.dk.com

MIX
Paper | Supporting
responsible forestry
FSC
www.fsc.org
FSC™ C018179

This book was made with Forest
Stewardship Council™ certified
paper – one small step in DK's
commitment to a sustainable future.
**For more information go to
www.dk.com/our-green-pledge**

Preface

This edition of *Hugo Italian in 3 Months* was written by Milena Reynolds, whose experience in teaching her native tongue ranges from beginners to post-graduate level. She has drawn on this expertise to produce a simple yet complete course for students working at home and aiming to acquire a good working knowledge of Italian in a short time. It is based on the Hugo principle of teaching only what is really essential for a firm grasp of practical, everyday language use.

The course begins with a detailed explanation of Italian pronunciation (our "imitated pronunciation" system will help you through the early stages). We strongly encourage you to download the free *DK Hugo In 3 Months* app (see p.4) and to listen to the accompanying audio—this will enable you to pick up the distinctive sounds of the Italian language.

The rest of the course is divided into 10 sections, each of which should take roughly a week to complete—so even if you proceed slightly more slowly than expected, you should still finish the course inside three months. Each section has a main theme divided into three or four related topics, presenting the grammar concisely and clearly, along with examples, exercises, and sample conversations. Ideally, you should spend about an hour a day on the course, although there is no hard and fast rule on this. Do as much as you feel capable of doing; it is better to learn a little at a time, and to learn that thoroughly.

At the beginning of each day's session, spend ten minutes going back over what you learned the day before. Study each new rule or numbered section carefully, to ensure you have fully understood the grammar and examples given, before listening to the audio to learn the pronunciation of sample sentences and new vocabulary. Then revisit each conversation and note how it uses the constructions that have been explained. With the conversations, we suggest that you listen to them first, then read them aloud and see how closely you can imitate the voices on the recording. Try to understand rather than memorize.

Finally, complete the exercises that accompany each section. Repeat them until the answers come easily. Repetition is vital to language learning. The more often you listen to a conversation or repeat an oral exercise, the faster your listening skills and fluency in speaking will improve.

When you've completed the course, you should have a very good understanding of the language – more than sufficient for general holiday or business purposes, and enough to support you in language validation tests if that is your aim. Remember that it is important to continue expanding your vocabulary by reading in Italian or watching Italian films—or, best of all, visiting Italy.

We hope you enjoy *Hugo Italian in 3 Months*, and we wish you success with your studies!

About the audio app

The audio app that accompanies this Italian course contains audio recordings for all the conversations, numbered sections, and vocabulary boxes, as well as many of the exercises. There is no audio for the Reading practice section.

◀✕ Where you see this symbol, it indicates that there is no audio for that section.

To start using the audio with this book, go to **www.dk.com/hugo** and download the *DK Hugo In 3 Months* app on your smartphone or tablet from the App Store or Google Play. Then, select Italian from the list of titles.

Please note that this app is not a stand-alone course. It is designed to be used together with the book, to familiarize you with Italian speech and to provide examples for you to repeat aloud.

Contents

Pronunciation

Before you start the first chapter, read the following rules on pronunciation. If you've downloaded the app, listen to the audio as you read the example words and sentences. Italian pronunciation is not too complicated, and once you've mastered the sounds that are different from English, you'll find that you can pronounce the words you learn quite easily. Our imitated pronunciation aims to help you with this until you get familiar with the sounds.

THE IMITATED PRONUNCIATION

In the first weeks of the course, the imitated pronunciation is included for each new word as it occurs in the sections or in the vocabulary list at the end of the chapter. In this system, the Italian sounds are represented phonetically; read each syllable as if it were part of an English word. After the third chapter, word stress will continue to be indicated for words in which the stress is <u>not</u> on the penultimate syllable. If in doubt, you can always come back to this section or listen to the audio.

When reading the imitated pronunciation, note that:

ah   sounds like a in father but is shorter than in English

oh   sounds like the o in bone or in hot

eh   sounds like the e in bed or the ay in say but much shorter

n'y   sounds like nyuh in onion

l'y   sounds like llyuh in million

rr   is rolled, something like a Scottish r

All new words appear in the vocabulary list at the end of each chapter. If you feel doubtful about the pronunciation, check the imitated pronunciation in the lists for the first three chapters.

STRESS

In Italian, most words end in a vowel and are generally stressed on the next-to-last syllable:

albergo [ahl-_bair_-goh] hotel
finito [fee-_nee_-toh] finished
idea [ee-_deh_-ah] idea

If the stress falls on the last vowel, that vowel will have a grave accent:

caffè [kahf-_fèh_] coffee
perché [paihr-_kày_] why

Sì (yes) has an accent because it might otherwise be confused with the word **si** (oneself), and **è** (is) is accented to distinguish it from **e** (and).

If the stress falls on the third-to-last syllable (or more rarely on the fourth-to-last), then we will underline the stressed vowel to indicate where to put the word stress:

timido [_tee_-mee-doh] shy
bellissimo [behl-_lees_-see-moh] very beautiful

The combinations **-ia, -io, -ie** at the end of a word are normally considered as a single syllable, so the stress falls on the preceding syllable:

Venezia [veh-_neh_-tsiah] Venice
doppio [_dohp_-pioh] double

Exceptions are marked by underlining the stressed vowel:

scrivania [skree-vah-_nee_-ah] desk

PRONUNCIATION OF VOWELS

The Italian vowels are **a, e, i, o**, and **u**. The vowels **o** and **e** can be open or closed according to the context.

a	is pronounced like a in father, but it is shorter in Italian	**sala** [sah-lah] hall
		la [lah] the
e	is pronounced like e in bed or like ay in say	**letto** [leht-toh] bed
		mela [may-lah] apple

i	is pronounced like ee in meet	**vino** [vee-noh] wine
o	is pronounced like o in not or like o in almost	**posta** [pos-tah] post **sono** [soh-noh] I am
u	is pronounced like oo in moon	**cura** [koo-rrah] cure

PRONUNCIATION OF CONSONANTS

Most consonants are pronounced like their English counterparts. The exceptions are:

c	is pronounced like ch in much before **e** and **i**, but it is pronounced like k in king before **o**, **a**, and **u**	**ci** [chee] there **casa** [kah-zah] house
ch	is always pronounced like k in king	**che** [keh] that
g	is pronounced like j in jeep before **e** and **i**, but it is pronounced like g in go before **a, o,** and **u**	**giro** [jee-rroh] trip **gara** [gah-rah] race **guida** [gwee-dah] guide
gh	is always pronounced like g in gate	**laghi** [lah-gee] lakes
gli	is pronounced like l'y in million	**luglio** [loo-l'yoh] July **gli** [l'yee] the
gn	is similar to n'y in companion	**ogni** [oh-n'yee] every **gnocchi** [n'yohk-kee] dumplings
h	is not pronounced at all	**ha** [ah] he has

qu	is pronounced like qu in queen	**qui** [qwee] here **questo** [qwehs-toh] this
r	is rolled or trilled, something like a Scottish r	**caro** [kah-rroh] dear
s	is as in see before consonants, when double, or at the beginning of words	**strada** [strah-dah] road **sesso** [sehs-soh] sex **sala** [sah-lah] hall
	but it is like z in lazy between two vowels	**casa** [kah-zah] home
sc	is pronounced like sh in she before **i** and **e**	**sci** [shee] ski **scena** [sheh-nah] scene
	but it is pronounced sk as in skip when followed by a consonant or by **o**, **a**, **u**	**scusa** [skoo-zah] sorry **scrivo** [skree-voh] I write
z	is pronounced like ts in gutsy	**pranzo** [prahn-tsoh] lunch
	or softer like dz at the beginning of words	**zero** [dzeh-rroh] zero

Double consonants are emphasized and pronounced as if there were a short pause in front of them:
ditta [deet-tah] firm, *but* **dita** [dee-tah] fingers
sonno [son-noh] sleep, *but* **sono** [soh-noh] I am

On the whole, when speaking Italian, you should linger on the vowels and not pronounce the consonants too forcefully (except in the case of double consonants). Remember at the end of a sentence to make your voice rise when it is a question and fall when it is a statement.

Week 1

You will learn:
- how to book a room in a hotel in Italian
- to introduce yourself and say where you come from
- to say hello and goodbye
- to use the formal form of address

The grammar includes:
- gender of nouns and adjectives
- the articles "the" (**il, lo, la, l'**) and "a" (**un, uno, una, un'**)
- negative sentences
- questions
- present tense of "to be" (**essere**) and "to have" (**avere**)
- present tense of regular **-are** verbs (**parlare**)

CONVERSATION 1

All'albergo

A dialogue between the hotel receptionist and Ms. Branson, who is booking a room.

MS. BRANSON	**Buongiorno.**
RECEPTIONIST	**Buongiorno, signora.**
MS. BRANSON	**Ha una camera libera?**
RECEPTIONIST	**Sì, certo, doppia o singola?**
MS. BRANSON	**Singola.**
RECEPTIONIST	**Per quanti giorni?**
MS. BRANSON	**Solo per oggi.**
RECEPTIONIST	**E il Suo nome, per favore?**
MS. BRANSON	**Sono Mary Branson.**
RECEPTIONIST	**È inglese?**
MS. BRANSON	**No, sono americana.**
RECEPTIONIST	**Ha un documento, per favore?**
MS. BRANSON	**Sì, ecco il passaporto.**
RECEPTIONIST	**Benissimo grazie, ecco la chiave.**

TRANSLATION 1

At the hotel

MS. BRANSON	Good morning.
RECEPTIONIST	Good morning, madam.
MS. BRANSON	Do you have a room [free]?
RECEPTIONIST	Yes, certainly, double or single?
MS. BRANSON	Single.
RECEPTIONIST	For how long [lit. "how many days"]?
MS. BRANSON	Only for today.
RECEPTIONIST	And your name, please?
MS. BRANSON	I'm Mary Branson.
RECEPTIONIST	Are you English?
MS. BRANSON	No, I'm American.
RECEPTIONIST	Do you have any identification [lit. "document"], please?
MS. BRANSON	Yes, here is my [lit. "the"] passport.
RECEPTIONIST	Fine, thank you, here is the key.

1.1 GENDER

All nouns (words that name things) in Italian are either masculine or feminine. For example, in the preceding conversation, **una camera** is feminine (f.), while **il passaporto** is masculine (m.). As a general rule, all nouns ending in **-a** are feminine, and all nouns ending in **-o** are masculine. There are exceptions, but we'll note these when we come across them.

Nouns ending in **-e** may be either masculine or feminine. So the best advice is to try to pay attention to and remember which article is used in front of a word:

il passaporto
la camera
la chiave
il signore

If there is an adjective (a descriptive word that qualifies the noun), this too will change according to the gender of the word to which it refers:

la signora americana
But
il passaporto americano

IMITATED PRONUNCIATION

eel pahs-sah-pohr-toh; lah k<u>ah</u>-meh-rrah;
lah kiah-veh; eel see-n'yoh-rreh;
lah see-n'yoh-rrah ah-meh-rree-kah-nah;
eel pahs-sah-pohr-toh ah-meh-rree-kah-noh

1.2 ARTICLES: A, AN, THE

"A" and "an" are translated in Italian by **un** before a masculine noun and **una** before a feminine noun.

Una takes an apostrophe (**un'**) before a feminine noun beginning with a vowel, and **un** becomes **uno** before words beginning with z or with s followed by another consonant:

una c<u>a</u>mera
un'americana
un albergo
uno studente

"The" is translated by **il** before masculine nouns beginning with consonants and **lo** before masculine nouns beginning with **z** or with **s** followed by another consonant. **La** is used before feminine words.

L' is used before both masculine and feminine words beginning with a vowel.

il nome
lo zero
l'albergo

la chiave
l'occupazione

IMITATED PRONUNCIATION

oon; oo-nah; oon; oo-noh; oo-nah k<u>ah</u>-meh-rrah;
oon ah-meh-rree-kah-nah; oon ahl-behr-goh;
oo-noh stoo-dehn-teh; eel; loh; lah; eel noh-meh;
loh dzeh-rroh; lahl-behr-goh; lah kiah-veh;
lok-koo-pah-tzioh-neh

1.3 QUESTIONS

When you want to ask a question in Italian, you simply make your voice rise at the end of the sentence. The word order does not change.

Il Suo nome è inglese?
Is your name English?
Il Suo nome è inglese.
Your name is English.

Exercise 1

Answer the questions about Conversation 1 using:
Sì, è ... (Yes, he/she/it is ...) *or*
No, è ... (No, he/she/it is ...)
Example:
Question: Il receptionist dell'albergo è inglese? (Is the hotel receptionist English?)
Answer: No, è italiano. (No, he is Italian.)

1 Mary Branson è americana? Sì, è ...
2 L'albergo è inglese? No, è ...
3 La camera è libera?
4 Il passaporto è americano?
5 La camera è solo per oggi?
6 Il receptionist dell'albergo è italiano?
7 La signora è inglese?
8 L'albergo è italiano?
9 La camera è singola?
10 La camera è doppia?

IMITATED PRONUNCIATION

eel soo-oh noh-meh eh in-gleh-zeh; see; noh;
rreh-sehp-syohn-eest; ee-tah-liah-nah; lee-beh-rrah;
seen-goh-lah; dohp-piah

1.4 NEGATIVE SENTENCES

In Italian, you make a sentence negative by putting **non** in front of the verb:

La signora non è inglese.
The lady is not English.
Mary non parla italiano.
Mary does not speak Italian.

Exercise 2

Make these sentences negative (in the exercises, use the vocabulary list at the end of each chapter for words you don't know):

1 Sono di Verona.
2 Sandro Bianchi ha una bella casa.
3 L'albergo è pieno.
4 La signorina lavora in un albergo.
5 Parlate bene l'italiano?

Exercise 3

Put the correct form of il, lo, l', la before the following words:

1 Questo è ... zoo.
2 Parliamo bene ... italiano.
3 ... marito di Mary è inglese
4 Rita è ... moglie di Sandro.
5 Ascolto ... opera alla Scala.
6 ... signora è italiana.
7 ... albergo è molto comodo.
8 Questa è ... camera singola.
9 Ecco ... chiave.
10 Ecco ... passaporto.

IMITATED PRONUNCIATION

nohn; pahr-lah; soh-noh; be-ahn-kee; behl-lah; kah-zah; pieh-noh; see-n'yoh-rree-nah; lah-voh-rrah; pahr-lah-teh; beh-neh; ee-tah-liah-noh; qwehs-toh; dzoh-oh; pahr-liah-moh; mah-rree-toh; moh-l'yeh; ahs-kohl-toh; oh-peh-hrah; koh-moh-doh; qwes-tah; ehk-koh

CONVERSATION 2

Al bar dell'albergo

A conversation between Mary Branson, her husband, Peter, and Paolo and Anna Rossi, an Italian couple also staying at the hotel.

MARY **Buongiorno.**
PAOLO **Buongiorno, signora.**
MARY **Mi chiamo Mary Branson.**
PAOLO **Piacere! Io sono Paolo Rossi.**
MARY **Piacere! Molto lieta!**
PAOLO **Questa è mia moglie.**
ANNA **Piacere!**
MARY **E questo è mio marito.**
PAOLO **Molto lieto! Parla italiano anche Lei?**
PETER **No.**
MARY **Purtroppo no. Siamo americani.**
PAOLO **Di dove siete?**
MARY **Siamo di Washington. E voi?**
PAOLO **Siamo di Milano.**
MARY **Ah! Milano è molto bella.**
ANNA **Sì, ma anche Washington è una città bella e famosa.**

TRANSLATION 2

At the hotel bar

MARY   Good morning.
PAOLO Good morning, madam.
MARY   My name is Mary Branson.
PAOLO Pleased to meet you. I'm Paolo Rossi.
MARY   Nice to meet you. It's a real pleasure.
PAOLO This is my wife.
ANNA   Pleased to meet you.
MARY   And this is my husband.
PAOLO Nice to meet you. Do you speak Italian, too?
PETER No.
MARY   Unfortunately not. We are American.
PAOLO Where are you from?
MARY   Washington. And you?
PAOLO We're from Milan.
MARY   Ah, Milan is very beautiful.
ANNA   Yes, but Washington is also a beautiful and
       famous city.

1.5 PRESENT TENSE OF **ESSERE** (TO BE)

1st sing.	**(io)**	**sono**	I am
2nd	**(tu)**	**sei**	you (familiar) are
3rd	**(lui, lei, Lei)**	**è**	he, she, it is; you (formal) are
1st pl.	**(noi)**	**siamo**	we are
2nd	**(voi)**	**siete**	you (plural) are
3rd	**(loro)**	**sono**	they are

NOTE: It is not necessary to use the subject pronouns **io**, **tu**, **Lei**, **lui**, **noi**, **voi**, or **loro**, except for emphasis.

IMITATED PRONUNCIATION

(ee-oh) soh-noh; (too) seh-ee; (loo'ee/leh'ee) eh; (no-ee) see-ah-moh; (vo-ee) see-eh-teh; (loh-rroh) soh-noh

1.6 FORMS OF ADDRESS

In Italian, there are two forms of address. When talking to children, friends, and family, the familiar form is used: **tu**. Although today Italians are quick to switch to **tu**, when addressing people you don't know well, it is polite to use the **Lei** form, which is in fact the third-person singular of the verb. When addressing more than one person, **voi** is used for both the formal and familiar forms:

Are you English?	**Sei inglese?**	(familiar singular)
	È inglese?	(formal)
	Siete inglesi?	(formal and familiar plural)

NOTE: Capital letters are used for **Lei, Suo/Sua**, etc. when they mean "you" and "yours" (formal), to distinguish them from **lei, suo/sua**, etc., which mean "she" and "his/hers."

1.7 PRESENT TENSE OF **AVERE** (TO HAVE)

ho	I have
hai	you have
ha	you (formal) have; he, she, it has
abbiamo	we have
avete	you (plural) have
hanno	they have

1.8 PRESENT TENSE OF **-ARE** VERBS

parlare (to speak)

parlo	I speak
parli	you speak
parla	you (formal) speak; he, she, it speaks
parliamo	we speak
parlate	you speak
parlano	they speak

1

All the regular verbs ending in -**are** are conjugated like **parlare** (e.g., **abitare, lavorare, ascoltare**).

NOTE: The stress moves to the ending in the first- and second-person plural [pahr-liah-moh, pahr-lah-teh] but reverts to the stem in the third-person plural [pahr-lah-noh].

IMITATED PRONUNCIATION

oh; ah'ee; ah; ahb-be-ah-moh; ah-veh-teh;
ahn-noh; pahr-lah-rreh; pahr-loh; pahr-lee;
pahr-lah; pahr-liah-moh; pahr-lah-teh; pahr-lah-noh;
ah-bee-tah-rreh; lah-voh-rrah-rreh; ahs-kohl-tah-rreh

CONVERSATION 3

In casa Brazzi

Mary and John White have been invited to Sandro and Rita Brazzi's flat in Venice after meeting them at a hospitality industry trade fair. They talk about what they do and where they live.

RITA	**Buonasera, John.**
JOHN	**Buonasera.**
RITA	**Questo è mio marito, Sandro.**
SANDRO	**Piacere.**
JOHN	**Questa è mia moglie, Mary.**
SANDRO	**Molto lieto, Mary.**
RITA	**Siete americani vero?**
MARY	**Sì, siamo di New York. E voi?**
RITA	**Siamo di Milano, ma abitiamo qui a Venezia da molti anni.**
SANDRO	**E a New York dove abitate?**
JOHN	**A Brooklyn.**
RITA	**Avete un appartamento o una casa?**
MARY	**Abbiamo una piccola casa con giardino.**
JOHN	**Sandro lavora a Venezia?**

RITA **Sì, ha un ristorante vicino a Piazza San Marco.**
MARY **Io sono insegnante. E tu?**
RITA **Io sono giornalista. E tuo marito?**
MARY **Lavora in un albergo nel centro di New York City.**

TRANSLATION 3

At the Brazzis'

RITA Good evening, John.
JOHN Good evening.
RITA This is my husband, Sandro.
SANDRO Nice to meet you.
JOHN This is my wife, Mary.
SANDRO Very pleased to meet you, Mary.
RITA You're American, aren't you?
MARY Yes, we're from New York. And you?
RITA We're from Milan, but we've lived (lit. "we live") in Venice for many years.
SANDRO And where do you live in New York?
JOHN In Brooklyn.
RITA Do you have an apartment or a house?
MARY We have a small house with a garden.
JOHN Does Sandro work in Venice?
RITA Yes, he has a restaurant near Piazza San Marco.
MARY I'm a teacher. And you?
RITA I'm a journalist. And your husband?
MARY He works in a hotel in the center of New York City.

Exercise 4

Read Conversation 3, then answer the following questions:

1 John è inglese?
2 Come si chiama sua moglie?
3 Dove abita Sandro?
4 Di dove sono Sandro e sua moglie?
5 Chi lavora a Venezia?
6 John lavora?
7 La moglie di Sandro è giornalista?
8 John lavora a Brooklyn?
9 Chi è insegnante?
10 Mary e John abitano in una casa con giardino?

Exercise 5

Translate:

1 I live in Milan.
2 Do you (formal) work in Venice?
3 Where do you (formal) live?
4 I am a journalist.
5 Rita Rossi speaks Italian.
6 We live in Pavia and work in Milan.
7 New York City is beautiful.
8 Do you (plural) have an (use "the") American passport?
9 Where do you (plural) come from?
10 I am American.

Try to remember these key phrases to help you recall the main grammatical points and topics of this chapter:

Ha una camera libera?
Sono di New York City.
Abito a Brooklyn.
Lavoro in centro.
Parlo un po' l'italiano.

The words listed below have all appeared in the exercises, conversations, or example phrases this week. Check how well you remember them by covering up one column or the other and translating them. All the adjectives are given in their masculine singular form.

a [ah]	at, to, in
abitare [ah-bee-tah-rreh]	to live
albergo (m.) [ahl-behr-goh]	hotel
americano/a [ah-meh-rree-kah-noh/nah]	American (m./f.)
anche [ahn-keh]	also, too
anno (m.) [ahn-noh]	year
appartamento (m.) [ahp-pahr-tah-mehn-toh]	apartment
ascoltare [ahs-kohl-tah-rreh]	to listen
avere [ah-veh-rreh]	to have
bello [behl-loh]	beautiful
benissimo [beh-nees-see-moh]	very well
buonasera [bwoh-nah-seh-rrah]	good evening
buongiorno [bwohn-johr-noh]	good morning
camera (f.) [kah-meh-rrah]	room
cameriere/a [kah-meh-rrieh-rreh/rrah]	waiter / waitress
casa (f.) [kah-zah]	home, house
centro (m.) [chen-troh]	center
certo [chehr-toh]	sure, certainly
chi [kee]	who
chiave (f.) [kiah-veh]	key
cognome (m.) [koh-n'yoh-meh]	family name

come [koh-meh]	how
commesso/a [kohm-mehs-soh/sah]	shop assistant
comodo [k<u>oh</u>-moh-doh]	comfortable
da molti anni	for many years
[dah mohl-tee ahn-nee]	
di [dee]	of
di dove [dee doh-veh]	where from
documento (m.)	document
[doh-koo-mehn-toh]	
doppio [dohp-pioh]	double
dove [doh-veh]	where
e [eh]	and
ecco [ehk-koh]	here's, here it is
essere [<u>eh</u>s-seh-rreh]	to be
famoso [fah-moh-zoh]	famous
giornalista [johr-nah-lees-tah]	journalist (m./f.)
giorno (m.) [johr-noh]	day
grazie [grah-tzieh]	thank you
il (m.) [eel]	the
inglese [in-gleh-zeh]	English (m./f.)
insegnante [in-seh-n'yan-teh]	teacher (m./f.)
italiano/a [ee-tah-liah-noh/nah]	Italian (m./f.)
la (f.) [lah]	the
lavorare [lah-voh-rrah-rreh]	to work
Lei [lay]	you (sing. formal)
lei (f.)	she
libero [l<u>ee</u>-beh-rroh]	free
lo [loh]	the
marito [mah-rree-toh]	husband
mi chiamo [mee kiah-moh]	my name is
Milano (f.) [mee-lah-noh]	Milan
mio [mee-oh]	my, mine
moglie (f.) [moh-l'yeh]	wife
molto [mohl-toh]	very, much
molto lieto/a	pleased (to meet you)
[mohl-toh lieh-toh/tah]	(m./f.)
no [noh]	no
nome (m.) [noh-meh]	name
non [nohn]	not
occupazione (f.)	job, occupation
[ok-koo-pah-tzioh-neh]	

oggi [od-jee]	today
opera (f.) [<u>oh</u>-peh-rrah]	opera
parlare [pahr-lah-rreh]	to speak
passaporto (m.) [pahs-sah-pohr-toh]	passport
Pavia (f.) [pah-<u>vee</u>-ah]	Pavia
per [pehr]	for
per favore [pehr fah-voh-rreh], **per piacere** [pehr piah-cheh-rreh]	please
piacere [piah-cheh-rreh]	pleased to meet you
piccolo [<u>pee</u>k-koh-loh]	small
pieno [pieh-noh]	full
purtroppo [poohr-trop-poh]	unfortunately
quanto [qwahn-toh]	how, how much
questo [qwehs-toh]	this
qui [qwee]	here
ristorante (m.) [rrees-toh-rran-teh]	restaurant
receptionist [rreh-sehp-syohn-eest]	receptionist (m./f.)
sì [see]	yes
si chiama [see kiah-mah]	he/she is called
signora (f.) [see-n'yoh-rrah]	Mrs., Ms., madam
signore (m.) [see-n'yoh-rreh]	Mr., sir
signorina (f.) [see-n'yoh-rree-nah]	Miss, young lady
singolo [s<u>ee</u>n-goh-loh]	single
solo [soh-loh]	only
specialmente [speh-chahl-mehn-teh]	specially
studente/ssa [stoo-dehn-teh/teh-sah]	student (m./f.)
Suo, Sua [soo-oh, soo-ah]	your, yours
un, uno, una [oon, oo-noh, oo-nah]	a, an
un po' [oon poh]	a little
Venezia (f.) [veh-neh-tsiah]	Venice
vero [veh-rroh]	true
vicino [vee-chee-noh]	near
zero (m.) [dzeh-rroh]	zero, nought
zoo (m.) [dzoh-oh]	zoo

Week 2

You will learn to:
- talk about your home, daily routine, family, and the rooms in a house
- talk about renting an apartment

The grammar includes:
- plurals of articles, nouns, and adjectives
- present tense of **-ere** and **-ire** verbs: **vivere** ("to live") and **dormire** ("to sleep")
- possessive adjectives and pronouns: **mio, tuo**, etc. ("my," "mine," "yours," etc.)
- **C'è** ("there is") and **ci sono** ("there are")
- prepositions: **a, da, di, in, su**
- possession
- question words: **che?** ("what?"), **di chi?** ("whose?"), **dove?** ("where?")

CONVERSATION 1

In una famiglia italiana

A conversation between the Italian host, signora Silvestri, and her guest, an English student, Peter Taylor

SILVESTRI	**Buongiorno signor Taylor, e benvenuto a casa nostra.**
TAYLOR	**Buongiorno signora Silvestri, piacere di conoscerla. È questa la mia camera?**
SILVESTRI	**Sì. È un po' piccola ma ha tutti i mobili necessari. E dalla finestra vede anche il Colosseo.**
TAYLOR	**Sì, sì! Mi piace, è luminosa e ha anche una scrivania per tutti i miei libri.**
SILVESTRI	**Tutti i miei ospiti prendono la prima colazione qui. Va bene anche per Lei?**
TAYLOR	**Sì, benissimo. E, scusi, dov'è il bagno per favore?**
SILVESTRI	**È in fondo al corridoio a destra.**
TAYLOR	**Dove metto la mia valigia?**
SILVESTRI	**Nello sgabuzzino vicino alla cucina.**
TAYLOR	**Grazie signora. Adesso metto via la mia roba.**

TRANSLATION 1

With an Italian family

SILVESTRI Good morning, Mr. Taylor, and welcome to
           our house.
TAYLOR   Good morning, Mrs. Silvestri, pleased to meet you.
           Is this my room?
SILVESTRI Yes, it's a little small but has all the furniture you
           need. And from the window you can see the
           Colosseum.
TAYLOR   Oh, yes! I like it. It's bright and even has a desk for
           all my books.
SILVESTRI All my guests have (lit. "take") their breakfast
           here. Is that all right with you?
TAYLOR   Yes, great. And, excuse me, where is the
           bathroom, please?
SILVESTRI At the end of the corridor on the right.
TAYLOR   Where can I put (lit. "I put") my suitcase?
SILVESTRI In the closet near the kitchen.
TAYLOR   Thank you. Now I'll put ("I put") my things away.

Exercise 1

Answer the following questions about Conversation 1:

1 La camera di Peter è grande?
2 Dov'è il bagno?
3 La signora Silvestri offre la colazione ai suoi ospiti?
4 Dove mette la valigia Peter?
5 Dov'è lo sgabuzzino?

2.1 MR., MRS., MISS, MS.

Note that **signore**, **signora**, and **signorina** take the definite article when they are followed by a name. Note also that **signore** becomes **signor**:

Il signor Bianchi è italiano.
Mr. Bianchi is Italian.
La signorina Rossi è qui.
Miss Rossi is here.

But in direct speech, these articles are not used:

Buongiorno, signora Rossi.
Good morning, Mrs. Rossi.

There is no equivalent to Ms. in Italian, but it has now become customary to address all women as **signora**. **Signorina** is used for very young women only.

2.2 PLURALS OF ARTICLES

The Italian definite articles **il**, **lo**, **la**, **l'** ("the") change in the plural:

	singular	plural
masculine	**il**	**i**
	lo, l'	**gli**
feminine	**la, l'**	**le**

IMITATED PRONUNCIATION

see-n'yohr; qwee; bwohn-johr-noh; eel, ee; loh, l'yee; lah, leh

2.3 PLURALS OF NOUNS AND ADJECTIVES

To make a noun plural, instead of adding "-s" as in English, you have to change its ending:

	singular	plural
masculine	**il libro**	**i libri**
	the book	the books
	lo studente	**gli studenti**
	the student	the students
	l'ingresso	**gli ingressi**
	the hall	the halls
feminine	**la camera**	**le camere**
	the room	the rooms
	l'ora	**le ore**
	the hour	the hours

This rule also applies to adjectives:

la camera ammobiliata   **le camere ammobiliate**
the furnished room   the furnished rooms
il signore inglese   **i signori inglesi**
the English gentleman   the English gentlemen
la signorina inglese   **le signorine inglesi**
the young English lady   the young English ladies

To help you remember this rule, here are the endings:

singular	plural
-o	**-i**
-e	**-i**
-a	**-e**

Note that all masculine and feminine nouns and adjectives ending in **-e** in the singular end in **-i** in the plural. Consequently, the endings of the noun and the adjective don't always match:

la casa grande   **le case grandi**
the big house   the big houses

IMITATED PRONUNCIATION

eel lee-broh, ee lee-bree; loh stoo-dehn-teh,
l'yee stoo-dehn-tee; leen-gres-soh, l'yee een-gres-see;
lah k<u>ah</u>-meh-rrah, leh k<u>ah</u>-meh-rreh; loh-rrah,
leh oh-rreh; lah k<u>ah</u>-meh-rrah ahm-moh-beel-yah-tah,
leh k<u>ah</u>-meh-rreh ahm-moh-beel-yah-teh;
eel see-n'yoh-rreh in-gleh-zeh,
ee see-n'yoh-rree in-gleh-zeh;
lah see-n'yoh-rree-nah in-gleh-zeh,
leh see-nyoh-rree-neh in-gleh-zee;
lah kah-zah grahn-deh, leh kah-zeh grahn-dee

Exercise 2

Make the following sentences plural.

Example:

Questo è il nostro libro. *Plural*: Questi sono i nostri libri.
Io guardo il giornale. *Plural*: Noi guardiamo i giornali.

1 Questa è la mia c<u>a</u>mera.

2 Il bagno è occupato.

3 Io lavoro per la mia compagn<u>i</u>a.

4 Lo studente americano studia molto.

5 La sua valigia è vuota.

6 Il pasto comincia dopo le nove.

7 Il nostro pensionante parla bene la lingua.

8 La signora arriva con la figlia.

9 Se la porta è aperta io entro.

10 L'appartamento al primo piano è spazioso.

IMITATED PRONUNCIATION

All the new words in this exercise can be found in the
vocabulary list at the end of the chapter. You can check
the imitated pronunciation there should you be in any
doubt. The same applies to the exercises that follow.

La nuova casa

Maria has just moved into her new apartment and describes it to her friend Luigi.

2

LUIGI   **Allora, sei contenta della tua nuova casa?**

MARIA   **Sì, abbastanza. Non è molto grande, ma almeno ci sono due camere da letto per i bambini.**

LUIGI   **Quante stanze avete in tutto?**

MARIA   **Tre camere da letto, la sala, il tinello, la cucina e il bagno.**

LUIGI   **E avete anche un bel terrazzo, vero?**

MARIA   **Sì, siamo al quarto piano con un grande terrazzo sul davanti e una sala abbastanza spaziosa.**

LUIGI   **Che bello! Così potete mangiar fuori d'estate.**

MARIA   **Appunto. E desideriamo invitare tutti i nostri amici il prossimo weekend. Venite anche voi, vero?**

LUIGI   **Certo, molto volentieri. Scrivi qui il tuo nuovo indirizzo. Vivete lontano dal centro?**

MARIA   **Sì, viviamo in periferia, ma c'è la metropolitana vicino.**

LUIGI   **Benissimo. Allora a sabato, ciao.**

MARIA   **Ciao Luigi. Arrivederci.**

TRANSLATION 2

The new home

LUIGI   Are you happy in your new home, then?

MARIA   Yes, quite. It's not very big, but at least there are two bedrooms for the children.

LUIGI   How many rooms do you have altogether?

MARIA   Three bedrooms, a dining room, breakfast room, kitchen, and bathroom.

LUIGI   And you have a beautiful terrace, don't you?

MARIA   Yes, we are on the fourth floor, with a large terrace at the front and a fairly big dining room.

LUIGI   How lovely! So you can eat outside in the summer.

MARIA   Exactly. And next weekend, we want to invite all our friends. You'll come (lit. "you [pl.] come"), too, won't you?

LUIGI   Yes, gladly. Write your new address here. Do you live far from the center?

MARIA   Yes, we live in the suburbs, but the metro is (lit. "there is the metro") nearby.

LUIGI   Good. See you Saturday then. Goodbye.

MARIA   Bye, Luigi. See you soon.

Exercise 3

Answer the following questions about Conversation 2:

1 Quante camere da letto ha l'appartamento di Maria?
2 A che piano è?
3 Che cosa fa Luigi il prossimo weekend?
4 Maria vive vicino al centro?
5 C'è la metropolitana vicino alla casa di Maria?

Exercise 4

You live in a small house on the outskirts of London, with two bedrooms, a large kitchen, and a big garden. Describe this to your business acquaintance signor Bianchi (B), who is planning to come to visit you.

Fill in the gaps with the correct form of the words given in brackets:

B   Lei abita a Londra, vero?

YOU   Sì, ma non in centro … *(I live in the suburbs).*

B   Ah, è difficile venire a casa Sua?

YOU   No, … *(there is the underground nearby).*

B   È una casa o un appartamento?

YOU   È … *(a small house with a large garden).*

B   In Inghilterra ci sono molte di queste case?

YOU   Sì, al pianterreno c'è … *(a large kitchen).*

B   E al primo piano che cosa c'è?

YOU   Ci sono … *(two bedrooms and a bathroom).*

B   Ma la vostra casa non è troppo lontana dall'ufficio?

YOU   No, … *(it is quite near).*

B   Siete proprio fortunati!

2.4   PRESENT TENSE OF -ERE AND -IRE VERBS

Italian verbs ending in **-ere** and **-ire** in the infinitive have very similar endings in the present tense:

	vivere (to live)	**dormire** (to sleep)
io	vivo	dormo
tu	vivi	dormi
Lei, lei, lui	vive	dorme
noi	viviamo	dormiamo
voi	vivete	dormite
loro	vivono	dormono

Other Italian verbs like **vivere** are **prendere** (to take), **vedere** (to see), and **scrivere** (to write). Verbs ending in **-ire** that conjugate like **dormire** are **sentire** (to hear), **vestire** (to dress), and **aprire** (to open).

There are many irregular verbs ending in **-ere** and **-ire**; we'll explain them as they appear in the course.

IMITATED PRONUNCIATION

vee-veh-rreh; vee-voh; vee-vee; vee-veh;
vee-vee-ah-mo; vee-veh-teh; vee-voh-noh;
dohr-mee-rreh; dohr-moh; dohr-mee; dohr-meh;
dohr-mee-ah-moh, dohr-mee-teh; dohr-moh-noh;
prehn-deh-rreh; skree-veh-rreh; sehn-tee-rreh;
vehs-tee-rreh; ah-pree-rreh

Exercise 5

Complete the following sentences using the correct present tense of the verb given in brackets:

1 La signora Bianchi (vivere) in periferia.
2 I bambini (dormire) in una piccola camera da letto.
3 Noi (prendere) il treno.
4 Voi (sentire) molto rumore dalla strada?
5 E tu perchè non (aprire) la finestra?
6 Voi (vedere) molti film alla televisione?
7 Gianni e Maria (vestire) con molta eleganza.
8 Voi non (sentire) mai il campanello.
9 Dove (mettere) le valigie lo studente?
10 Noi (conoscere) Firenze molto bene.

2.5 MY, MINE, YOUR, YOURS, ETC.

In order to establish ownership, you use these possessive adjectives and pronouns:

	m. sing.	f. sing.	m. pl.	f. pl.
my, mine	**mio**	**mia**	**miei**	**mie**
your, yours (*fam.*)	**tuo**	**tua**	**tuoi**	**tue**
his, her, hers, its	**suo**	**sua**	**suoi**	**sue**
your, yours (*form.*)	**Suo**	**Sua**	**Suoi**	**Sue**
our, ours	**nostro**	**nostra**	**nostri**	**nostre**
your, yours (*pl.*)	**vostro**	**vostra**	**vostri**	**vostre**
their, theirs	**il loro**	**la loro**	**i loro**	**le loro**

NOTE: All these adjectives and pronouns need to agree with the gender and number of the thing <u>possessed</u>, not with the possessor:

| **la sua casa** | his house |
| **i miei libri** | my books |

Note also that in Italian, they are preceded by an article:

| **la nostra camera** | our room |
| **i vostri pensionanti** | your lodgers |

BUT, with most of them, the article is omitted before a member of the family in the singular:

| **mio marito** | my husband |
| **sua moglie** | his wife |

Loro, however, is always used with an article:

| **il loro padre** | their father |

IMITATED PRONUNCIATION

mee-oh, mee-ah, mee-eh'ee, mee-eh; too-oh, too-ah,
too-oh'ee, too-eh; soo-oh, soo-ah, soo-oh'ee, soo-eh;
nohs-troh, nohs-trah, nohs-tree, nohs-treh; vohs-troh,
vohs-trah, vohs-tree, vohs-treh; eel lohr-roh,
lah lohr-roh, ee lohr-roh, leh lohr-roh

Exercise 6

Complete the following sentences using the correct
form of the possessive adjectives with or without the
articles, as explained in section 2.5. Look at the
conjugation of the verb to know which form of "you"
to use (formal, familiar, singular, or plural).

Example:
Questa è (my) camera. Questa è la mia camera.
Questa è (my) moglie. Questa è mia moglie.

1 Oggi invitiamo Mario e (his) figli.

2 (her) appartamento è al terzo piano.

3 I Bianchi vivono con (their) famiglia.

4 Vivete ancora con (your) genitori?

5 Ho un appuntamento con (my) amici.

6 Vivi con (your) madre?

7 Signora, Lei conosce (our) ditta?

8 Questo è (my) padre.

9 Signor Bianchi, dove sono (your) valigie?

10 Signori, sono queste (your) valigie?

Un appartamento da affittare

Ms. Smith needs to rent an apartment in Naples. She has found one and wants to find out from the landlord, signor Piani, as much as possible about the location, amenities, etc.

2

PIANI **Abbiamo un appartamento ammobiliato libero in luglio.**

SMITH **Dov'è l'appartamento?**

PIANI **È vicino al centro di Napoli.**

SMITH **C'è una scuola vicino? Perché i miei figli vanno ancora a scuola.**

PIANI **Sì, ci sono le scuole elementari e anche una scuola media.**

SMITH **C'è un garage per la nostra macchina?**

PIANI **Sì, ma l'affitto del garage è extra.**

SMITH **Capisco. E quante stanze ci sono?**

PIANI **Tre camere da letto, la sala da pranzo, il tinello, una cucina moderna e due bagni.**

SMITH **A che piano è?**

PIANI **Al sesto piano, ma c'è l'ascensore.**

SMITH **L'appartamento è ammobiliato, vero? C'è tutto il necessario?**

PIANI **Sì, c'è la lavatrice, l'aspirapolvere, la lavapiatti e forniamo anche la biancheria se desidera.**

SMITH **Benissimo. Abbiamo noi la biancheria, ma i miei bambini chiedono se c'è anche la televisione.**

PIANI **Sì, certo.**

SMITH **Ci sono negozi lì vicino? Questo è importante per noi.**

PIANI **Sì, c'è un supermercato nella stessa strada e anche un mercato in Piazza Indipendenza.**

SMITH **È possibile avere le chiavi oggi per vedere l'appartamento?**

PIANI **Certo.**

An apartment to rent

2

PIANI   We have a furnished apartment free in July.

SMITH   Where is the apartment?

PIANI   Near the center of Naples.

SMITH   Is there a school nearby? Because my children are still at school.

PIANI   Yes, there are elementary schools and a middle school.

SMITH   Is there a garage for our car?

PIANI   Yes, but the rent for the garage is extra.

SMITH   I understand. How many rooms are there?

PIANI   Three bedrooms, a dining room, breakfast room, a modern kitchen, and two bathrooms.

SMITH   What floor is it on?

PIANI   On the sixth floor, but there's an elevator.

SMITH   The apartment is furnished, isn't it? Is everything provided?

PIANI   Yes, there's a washing machine, a vacuum cleaner, a dishwasher, and we provide bed linen if you wish.

SMITH   Good. We have bed linen, but my children want to know if there is a television as well.

PIANI   Yes, certainly.

SMITH   Are there local shops? That's important for us.

PIANI   Yes, there is a supermarket on the same road and also a market in Piazza Indipendenza.

SMITH   Is it possible to have the keys today to see the apartment?

PIANI   Certainly.

2.6 C'È (THERE IS) AND CI SONO (THERE ARE)

In the conversations, you may have noticed that when you want to use "there is" or "there are" in Italian, you use **c'è** and **ci sono**:

c'è un supermercato
there is a supermarket
ci sono negozi
there are shops

Note that **c'è** and **ci sono** retain the same form in a question and in the negative form:

C'è la metropolitana?   **No, non c'è.**
Is there a metro stop?   No, there isn't.
Ci sono negozi?   **Sì, ci sono molti negozi.**
Are there shops?   Yes, there are many shops.

IMITATED PRONUNCIATION

cheh; chee soh-noh; soo-pehr-mehr-kah-toh;
neh-goh-dzee; meh-troh-poh-lee-tah-nah

Exercise 7

Answer these questions concerning Conversation 3. You can answer yes or no, but give a full reply:

1 La signora Smith ha bambini?
2 L'affitto comprende il garage?
3 La signora desidera avere la biancheria?
4 Dov'è il mercato?
5 C'è tutto il necessario nell'appartamento?

2.7 PREPOSITIONS: TO, FROM, OF, AT, ETC.

The most commonly used prepositions are:

a	to, at
da	from, by
di	of
in	in, at
su	on

These prepositions stand on their own when they are followed by the indefinite article (**un**, **una**, **uno**, or **un**):

di una signora   **a un figlio**
of a lady   to a son

But when they are followed by the definite article (**il**, **lo**, **la**, **l'**, **i**, **gli**, **le**), the preposition and article combine to form one word. Below are all the forms of these contracted prepositions:

	m. sing.			f. sing.	
a	**al**	**allo**	**all'**	**alla**	**all'**
da	**dal**	**dallo**	**dall'**	**dalla**	**dall'**
di	**del**	**dello**	**dell'**	**della**	**dell'**
in	**nel**	**nello**	**nell'**	**nella**	**nell'**
su	**sul**	**sullo**	**sull'**	**sulla**	**sull'**

	m. pl.		f. pl.
a	**ai**	**agli**	**alle**
da	**dai**	**dagli**	**dalle**
di	**dei**	**degli**	**delle**
in	**nei**	**negli**	**nelle**
su	**sui**	**sugli**	**sulle**

These are the only prepositions that have a contracted form in modern Italian. All the other prepositions that we'll come across in this course stand separate from the following article:

per la ragazza   for the girl
con i miei figli   with my children

2.8 POSSESSION

In Italian, there is no equivalent of the English apostrophe + s (e.g., the student's room). Possession has to be expressed using "of (the)" (e.g., **di**, **del**, etc.):

the student's room   **la stanza dello studente**

These prepositions are also used in expressions such as:

the kitchen door   **la porta della cucina**

2.9 QUESTION WORDS: WHOSE? WHAT? WHERE?

To ask the question "whose?" in Italian, you say **di chi?**:

Di chi è questa casa?
Whose house is this?

"What?" is expressed by **che?** or **che cosa?** (often shortened to **cosa?**):

Che/Che cosa/Cosa desidera?
What do you want?

"Where" is expressed by **dove**:

Dove abita?
Where do you live?

Exercise 8

Answer the following questions using the correct form of the contracted prepositions del, dello, dell', della, dei, degli, delle:

Example:
Di chi è questa stanza? (ragazza) È della ragazza.
(Whose room is this?) (It's the girl's.)

1 Di chi è l'appartamento?
   (signor Rossi)
2 Di chi è la scrivania?
   (studenti)
3 Di chi è questo libro?
   (mio amico)
4 Di chi è la macchina?
   (signora Rossi)
5 Di chi è la camera?
   (bambini)

Exercise 9

Put the correct form of the contracted prepositions al, allo, all', alla, ai, agli, alle in the spaces provided:

Example:
La stazione è vicino ... parco. La stazione è vicino al parco.

1 Il ristorante è vicino ... zoo.
2 Il bar è vicino ... ristorante.
3 La sala è vicino ... cucina.
4 Il parco è vicino ... giardini.
5 La porta è vicino ... finestre.
6 I ragazzi sono vicino ... albergo.
7 I libri sono vicino ... studenti.

Exercise 10

Make the following sentences plural:

1 Trovo l'appartamento ammobiliato sul giornale.
2 La figlia della signora vive con il suo ragazzo.
3 Non vedo la differenza tra questa casa e l'altra.
4 La chiave della porta è dalla portinaia.
5 L'inquilino prende la cartolina dalla cassetta delle lettere.

Exercise 11

Make the following sentences singular:

1 Mettiamo la nostra macchina in garage.
2 Partiamo per l'ufficio da soli.
3 Scrivete a vostra sorella oggi?
4 I suoi fratelli vivono qui?
5 Sentono molti rumori nelle strade affollate.

Exercise 12

Translate the following sentences:

1 Maria lives with her father in Rome.
2 My apartment is near the center of Milan.
3 Whose bedroom is this? It's the children's.
4 Their kitchen is small.
5 Where do you (plural) live, in an apartment or (in) a house?

Try to remember these key phrases to help you recall the main grammatical points and topics of this chapter:

2

Dov'è il suo appartamento?
Quante stanze ci sono?
Di chi è questo?
Mio marito e i miei figli vivono in Italia.

The words listed below have all appeared in this week's exercises, conversations, and examples. Check how well you remember them by covering up one column or the other and translating them.

abbastanza [ahb-bas-tahn-tsah]	quite, enough
affitto (m.) [ahf-feet-toh]	rent
affollato [ahf-fohl-lah-toh]	crowded
allegro [ahl-leh-groh]	cheerful
allora [ahl-loh-rrah]	then
almeno [ahl-meh-noh]	at least
amico/a [ah-mee-koh/kah]	friend
amici/amiche [ah-mee-chee/cheh]	friends
ammobiliato [ahm-moh-beel-yah-toh]	furnished
anche [ahn-keh]	also, too, as well
ancora [ahn-koh-rrah]	still, again, yet
aperto [ah-pehr-toh]	open
appuntamento (m.) [ahp-poon-tah-mehn-toh]	appointment
appunto [ahp-poon-toh]	precisely, exactly
aprire [ah-pree-rreh]	to open
arrivederci [ahr-ree-veh-dehr-chee]	bye, goodbye
aspirapolvere (m.) [ahs-pee-rrah-pohl-veh-rreh]	vacuum cleaner
bagno (m.) [bah-n'yoh]	bathroom
bambino/a [bahm-bee-noh/nah]	child
benvenuto/a/i/e [behn-veh-noo-toh/tah/tee/teh]	welcome (to a male, female, m. pl., f. pl.)
biancheria (f.) [biahn-keh-rree-ah]	bed linen
camera da letto (f.) [kah-meh-rrah dah leht-toh]	bedroom

cartolina (f.) [kahr-toh-lee-nah] — postcard
cassetta delle lettere (f.) — mailbox
  [kahs-set-tah dehl-leh leht-teh-rreh]
che, che cosa [keh koh-zah] — what
chiedere [kyeh-deh-rreh] — to ask
ciao [chao] — hello, goodbye
colazione (f.) [koh-lah-tzioh-neh] — breakfast
compagnia (f.) [kom-pah-n'yee-ah] — company
contento [kohn-tehn-toh] — happy
corridoio (m.) [kohr-rree-doy-oh] — corridor
così [koh-zee] — so, like this
cucina (f.) [koo-chee-nah] — kitchen
da [dah] — from, by
davanti a [dah-vahn-tee ah] — in front of
desiderare [deh-zee-deh-rrah-rreh] — to wish, to want
destra [dehs-trah] — right
differenza (f.) [deef-feh-rren-tsah] — difference
difficile [deef-fee-chee-leh] — difficult
ditta (f.) [deet-tah] — firm, company
dormire [dohr-mee-rreh] — to sleep
due [doo-eh] — two
estate (f.) [ehs-tah-teh] — summer
extra [ehks-trah] — extra
famiglia (f.) [fah-mee-l'yah] — family
figlio/a [fee-l'yoh/yah] — son, daughter, child
finestra (f.) [fee-nehs-trah] — window
fratello (m.) [frah-tehl-loh] — brother
fuori [fwoh-rree] — outside
garage (m.) [gah-rrah-jeh] — garage
genitori (m. pl.) [jeh-nee-toh-rree] — parents
giardino (m.) [jahr-dee-noh] — garden
giornale (m.) [johr-nah-leh] — newspaper
grande [grahn-deh] — big
importante [im-pohr-tahn-teh] — important
indirizzo (m.) [in-dee-rreedz-zoh] — address
in fondo a [in fohn-doh ah] — at the end of
inquilino/a [in-qwee-lee-noh/nah] — tenant
in tutto [in toot-toh] — altogether
invitare [in-vee-tah-rreh] — to invite
lavapiatti (f.) [lah-vah-piaht-tee] — dishwasher
lavatrice (f.) [lah-vah-tree-cheh] — washing machine

lingua (f.) [lin-gwah]	language
Londra (f.) [lohn-drah]	London
lontano da [lohn-tah-noh dah]	far from
luglio (m.) [loo-l'yoh]	July
ma [mah]	but
macchina (f.) [mahk-kee-nah]	car
madre (f.) [mah-dreh]	mother
mangiare [mahn-jah-rreh]	to eat
Metropolitana (f.) [meh-troh-poh-lee-tah-nah]	metro
mettere [meht-teh-rreh]	to put
mobili (m. pl.) [moh-bee-lee]	furniture
moderno [moh-dehr-noh]	modern
negozio (m.) [neh-goh-dzioh]	shop
occupato [ohk-koo-pah-toh]	busy
occupazione (f.) [ohk-koo-pah-dzioh-neh]	occupation
ospite (m. & f.) [ohs-pee-teh]	guest
padre (m.) [pah-dreh]	father
pasto (m.) [pahs-toh]	meal
pensionante (m. & f.) [pehn-sioh-nahn-teh]	paying guest
periferia (f.) [peh-rree-feh-rree-ah]	suburbs
piano (m.) [piah-noh]	floor, story
pianterreno (m.) [pian-tehr-reh-noh]	ground floor
piazza (f.) [piadz-zah]	public square
porta (f.) [pohr-tah]	door
portinaio/a [pohr-tee-nay-oh/ah]	doorkeeper, concierge
possibile [pohs-see-bee-leh]	possible
potere [poh-teh-rreh]	to be able
prendere [prehn-deh-rreh]	to take, to fetch
primo [pree-moh]	first
prossimo [prohs-see-moh]	next
quarto [qwahr-toh]	fourth
ragazzo/a [rrah-gadz-zoh/zah]	boy / girl (young person, age 15–25), boyfriend / girlfriend
roba (f.) [rroh-bah]	belongings, things
rumore (m.) [rroo-moh-rreh]	noise

sabato (m.) [s<u>ah</u>-bah-toh]	Saturday
sala da pranzo (f.)	dining room
[sah-lah dah prahn-dzoh]	
scrivania (f.) [skree-vah-n<u>ee</u>-ah]	desk
scrivere [skr<u>ee</u>-veh-rreh]	to write
scuola (f.) [sqwoh-lah]	school
scuola elementare (f.)	elementary school
[eh-leh-mehn-tah-rreh]	
scuola media (f.) [meh-diah]	middle school
sentire [sehn-tee-rreh]	to hear
sesto [sehs-toh]	sixth
sgabuzzino (m.)	storage room,
[sgah-boodz-zee-noh]	closet
sorella (f.) [soh-rrehl-lah]	sister
spazioso [spah-dzioh-zoh]	roomy
stanza (f.) [stahn-dzah]	room
su [soo]	on
supermercato (m.)	supermarket
[soo-pehr-mehr-kah-toh]	
televisione (f.)	television
[teh-leh-vee-zioh-neh]	
terrazzo (m.) [tehr-radz-zoh]	terrace
tinello (m.) [tee-nehl-loh]	breakfast room
tra [trah]	among, between
trovare [troh-vah-rreh]	to find
valigia (f.) [vah-lee-jah]	suitcase
vedere [veh-deh-rreh]	to see
vestire [vehs-tee-rreh]	to dress
vivere [v<u>ee</u>-veh-rreh]	to live
vuoto [vwoh-toh]	empty
weekend (m.) [week-end]	weekend
zio/a [dzee-oh/ah]	uncle / aunt

2

Week 3

You will learn to:
- ask the way
- ask about tickets
- talk about types of transportation
- find out times of arrivals and departures

The grammar will include:
- demonstrative adjectives & pronouns ("this," "that," "those")
- indefinite adjectives ("some," "any," etc.)
- numbers up to 1,000
- telling the time
- regular past participles and use of the present perfect tense
- irregular verbs: **andare** ("to go") and **fare** ("to do," "to make")

CONVERSATION 1

All'Ufficio del Turismo

Peter Taylor wants to get to know Rome and goes to the tourist office to ask the tourism officer, Carla Sacchi, for a map of the city and information about public transportation.

PETER   **Buongiorno. Scusi, ha una cartina di Roma?**

CARLA   **In inglese o in italiano?**

PETER   **In italiano, grazie. Studio l'italiano all'università e così imparo di più.**

CARLA   **Buon'idea. Eccola. Desidera qualche altra informazione?**
  [Peter apre la cartina]

PETER   **È questa l'università?**

CARLA   **No, quello è il politecnico. Questi sono gli istituti universitari.**

PETER   **Grazie, e c'è un autobus o la metropolitana?**

CARLA   **Dunque, vede qui sulla carta, questa è la metropolitana, e qui c'è la fermata dell'autobus.**

PETER   **Grazie mille. Dove compro i biglietti per l'autobus?**

CARLA   **Dal tabaccaio o dal giornalaio. Ogni biglietto è valido per settantacinque minuti.**

PETER   **Settantacinque minuti per qualsiasi distanza?**

CARLA   **Sì, anche quando cambia autobus.**

PETER   **Grazie. Arrivederci.**

CARLA   **Arrivederci e buon soggiorno.**

3

TRANSLATION 1

At the Tourist Office

PETER   Good morning. Do you have a map of Rome, please?

CARLA   In English or in Italian?

PETER   In Italian, please (lit. "thanks"). I'm studying Italian at the university, and that way I'll learn (lit. "like this I learn") more.

CARLA   Good idea! Here it is. Do you want any other information? [Peter opens the map]

PETER   Is this the university?

CARLA   No, that's the polytechnic. These are the university institutes.

PETER   Thank you. And is there a bus or a metro stop (lit. "the metro")?

CARLA   Well, you see here on the map, this is the metro, and here is the bus stop.

PETER   Thank you very much. Where can I buy (lit. "I buy") the tickets for the bus?

CARLA   At the tobacconist or newsdealer. Each ticket is valid for 75 minutes.

PETER   75 minutes whatever the distance?

CARLA   Yes, even when you change buses.

PETER   Thank you. Goodbye.

CARLA   Goodbye, and have a nice stay.

Exercise 1

Read or listen to Conversation 1 carefully, then answer the following questions:

1 Dove va Peter?
2 Che cosa desidera?
3 Dove compra i biglietti per l'autobus?
4 Per quanti minuti è valido un biglietto?

3

3.1 THIS, THAT, THOSE, ETC.

The demonstrative adjectives and pronouns "this" and "these" are:

questo   this (m. sing.)
questa   this (f. sing.)
questi   these (m. pl.)
queste   these (f. pl.)

These adjectives and pronouns need to agree with the noun they refer to:

questo autobus è in ritardo
this bus is late
questa è la Sua cartina
this is your map
questi sono gli istituti
these are the institutes
queste fermate sono obbligatorie
these are compulsory stops

"That" and "those" are a little more complicated:

quel, quell', quello	that (m. sing.)
quella, quell'	that (f. sing.)
quei, quegli	those (m. pl.)
quelle	those (f. pl.)

Note that the masculine forms have the same endings as the definite articles (**il, lo, l', i, gli**) according to whether the following word begins with a vowel or a consonant. So you use:

quel when you would use **il**
(before consonants)

quell' when you would use **l'**
(before vowels)

quello when you would use **lo**
(before **z**, **s** + consonant, **gn**)

quei when you would use **i**
(before consonants)

quegli when you would use **gli**
(before vowels, **z**, **s** + consonant, **gn**)

Examples:

Quel semaforo non funziona.
That traffic light doesn't work.

Quell'autobus è in orario.
That bus is on time.

Quello studente è inglese.
That student is English.

Quella motocicletta è pericolosa.
That motorcycle is dangerous.

Quell'automobile è guasta.
That car has (lit. "is") broken down.

Quei viaggiatori sono seduti.
Those travelers are seated.

Quegli sportelli sono aperti.
Those doors are open.

Quelle gomme sono sgonfie.
Those tires are flat.

BUT this is true of only demonstrative adjectives. The demonstrative pronouns (i.e., when **quello, quelli, quella,** and **quelle** are used on their own) have regular endings in the singular and in the plural:

Quello è l'ufficio informazioni.
That's the information office.

Quelli sono tutti posti prenotati.
Those are all reserved seats.

Note that these pronouns also express "the one/the ones" in English:

Quel posto è occupato. Prendo quello vicino al finestrino.
That seat is taken. I'll take the one near the window.

IMITATED PRONUNCIATION

kwehs-toh, kwehs-tah, kwehs-tee, kwehs-teh; <u>ow</u>-toh-boos; rree-tahr-doh; kahr-tee-nah; is-tee-too-tee; fehr-mah-teh; ohb-blee-gah-toh-rree-eh; kwehll; kwehl-loh; kwehl-lah; kweh'ee; kwehl-l'yee; kwehl-leh

For the pronunciation of any words not indicated above, check the vocabulary list at the end of this chapter. This also gives the meanings of new words in the exercises.

Exercise 2

Change the following sentences using quel, quell', quello, quella, quei, quegli, or quelle instead of the definite articles.
Example:
I treni sono veloci.→ Quei treni sono veloci.

1 La cartina è gratis.
2 L'autobus è affollato.
3 Il treno è veloce.
4 Lo scompartimento è riservato.
5 Partite con gli amici di Emma?
6 Porti le valigie in stazione?
7 I biglietti sono di andata e ritorno.
8 Gli orari non sono giusti.
9 Parti con l'aereo?
10 Sono liberi i posti?

Exercise 3

Translate the following sentences:

1 This is my seat.
2 These tickets are valid for three hours.
3 These are my Italian guests.
4 We take that train.
5 Is that the bus stop?
6 Those children are English.
7 We travel on that bus.
8 Those are my suitcases.
9 That [train] door is open.
10 This is the station.

3.2 INDEFINITE ADJECTIVES (SOME, ANY, ETC.)

The indefinite adjectives are **qualche** (some),
ogni (every), **qualsiasi/qualunque** (any, whatever).

ogni vagone
every/each carriage
qualche ora
some hours
qualsiasi distanza
whatever distance
qualunque autostrada
any motorway

Note: these indefinite adjectives are ALWAYS treated as
singular in Italian:

Qualche treno arriva in orario.
Some trains arrive on time.

IMITATED PRONUNCIATION

kwahl-keh; oh-n'yee; kwahl-see-ah-see; kwahl-oon-
kweh; vah-goh-neh; oh-rrah; dees-tahn-tzah; ow-toh-
strah-dah; treh-noh; oh-hrah-rrioh

Alla fermata dell'autobus

Peter is now at the bus stop waiting to catch the bus to the university. Signora Mazzi, who is also waiting there, starts talking to him.

3

SIGNORA	**Prende anche Lei il tredici?**
PETER	**Veramente non sono sicuro. Qual è l'autobus per l'università?**
SIGNORA	**Quello è il venticinque e passa ogni dieci minuti.**
PETER	**Scusi, che ore sono adesso?**
SIGNORA	**Sono le undici e mezzo.**
PETER	**Grazie, signora. E Lei dove va?**
SIGNORA	**Ho un appuntamento con mia figlia, in Piazza Navona a mezzogiorno.**
PETER	**Quanto ci vuole in autobus?**
SIGNORA	**Circa un quarto d'ora. Ma, vede quell'autobus? È il venticinque. È proprio fortunato Lei!**

TRANSLATION 2

At the bus stop

MS. MAZZI	Are you also taking the 13?
PETER	I'm not sure, actually. Which is the bus for the university?
MS. MAZZI	That's the 25, and there's one every 10 minutes.
PETER	What's the time, please?
MS. MAZZI	Half past eleven.
PETER	Thank you. Where are you going?
MS. MAZZI	I'm meeting (lit. "have an appointment with") my daughter in Piazza Navona at midday.
PETER	How long does it take by bus?
MS. MAZZI	About a quarter of an hour. But do you see that bus? It's the 25. You are really lucky!

Exercise 4

Read or listen to Conversation 2 several times, repeating after each speaker out loud. When you're ready, answer these questions:

1 Dove va l'autobus 13?
2 Che ore sono?
3 A che ora ha appuntamento la signora?
4 Quanto ci vuole per andare in Piazza Navona?
5 Che autobus va all'università?

3.3 NUMBERS

1	uno	16	sedici
2	due	17	diciassette
3	tre	18	diciotto
4	quattro	19	diciannove
5	cinque	20	venti
6	sei	30	trenta
7	sette	40	quaranta
8	otto	50	cinquanta
9	nove	60	sessanta
10	dieci	70	settanta
11	undici	80	ottanta
12	dodici	90	novanta
13	tredici	100	cento
14	quattordici	200	duecento
15	quindici	1,000	mille

NOTE: all numbers in Italian are written as one word. So:

23	ventitrè
197	centonovantasette
865	ottocentosessantacinque

BUT: when using tens and units, you drop the endings of **venti**, **trenta**, **quaranta**, etc. before **uno** and **otto**:

21	ventuno	31	trentuno
41	quarantuno	28	ventotto
38	trentotto	48	quarantotto

IMITATED PRONUNCIATION

oo-noh; doo-eh; treh; kwaht-troh; cheen-kweh; say'ee;
seht-teh; oht-toh; noh-veh; dee-ay-chee; oon-dee-chee;
doh-dee-chee; treh-dee-chee; kwaht-tohr-dee-chee;
kween-dee-chee; seh-dee-chee; dee-chahs-seht-teh;
dee-choht-toh; dee-chahn-noh-veh; vehn-tee;
trehn-tah; kwah-rrahn-tah; cheen-kwahn-tah;
sehs-sahn-tah; seht-tahn-tah; oht-tahn-tah;
noh-vahn-tah; chehn-toh; doo-eh-chehn-toh;
meel-leh; vehn-tee-treh; chehn-toh noh-vahn-tah
seht-teh; oht-toh chehn-toh sehs-sahn-tah cheen-kweh;
vehn-too-noh; vehn-toht-toh

3.4 TELLING THE TIME

To ask "What's the time?" in Italian, you say: **Che ore
sono?** or **Che ora è?** The answer is: **Sono le ...** followed
by the hour and then the minutes.

it is 5:30	**sono le cinque e mezzo**
it is 6:00	**sono le sei**
it is 6:15	**sono le sei e un quarto**
it is 6:45	**sono le sei e tre quarti**
it is 5:45	**sono le sei meno un quarto**
it is 6:05	**sono le sei e cinque**
it is 6:55	**sono le sei e cinquantacinque**
it is 5:55	**sono le sei meno cinque**

Note that the singular verb **è** is used with **mezzogiorno**
(midday), **mezzanotte** (midnight), and **l'una** (one o'clock):

it is midday	**è mezzogiorno**
it is midnight	**è mezzanotte**
it is one o'clock	**è l'una**

Note also that instead of indicating a time as "a.m." or
"p.m.", the 24-hour clock is often used in Italy:

it is 8:20 p.m.	**sono le venti e venti**

To ask "At what time ...?" (i.e., when something is going to happen), you say **A che ora ...?**:

A che ora parte l'autobus?
What time does the bus leave?
Alle quattro e mezzo.
At 4:30. (if on an official timetable, this would be a.m.!)
All'una.
At one o'clock.
A mezzanotte.
At midnight.

Exercise 5

Write down the time in Italian as in the examples below:

12:30   È mezzogiorno e mezzo.
 7:45   Sono le sette e tre quarti/Sono le otto meno un quarto.

1	2:30	**6**	4:45
2	3:00	**7**	8:35
3	21:00	**8**	1:30
4	12:15	**9**	2:50
5	24:00	**10**	7:10

Exercise 6

Change the following statements into questions using "A che ora ...?" and the answers. For example:

Il treno parte alle 8.   Question: A che ora parte il treno?
                          Answer: Alle otto.

1 L'autobus parte alle 6.

2 L'aereo parte alle 7.30.

3 Il treno parte alle 22.30.

4 Il treno arriva alle 17.25.

5 L'autobus arriva alle 13.15.

CONVERSATION 3

Alla stazione

Peter Taylor is at the Stazione Termini in Rome to meet his friend Luisa, who has just arrived from Siena.

PETER **Ciao Luisa, finalmente sei arrivata!**

LUISA **Scusa, Peter, ma il treno è partito in ritardo già da Siena.**

PETER **Non importa. Sei stanca adesso? A che ora sei partita da casa?**

LUISA **Sono partita da casa alle sei! Prima sono andata in bicicletta fino alla stazione e poi ho aspettato il treno per un'ora.**

PETER **Allora, andiamo subito a mangiare qualcosa. Ho già prenotato il ristorante.**

LUISA **Benissimo, grazie Peter. Hai avvisato la tua padrona di casa?**

PETER **Certo. E ha già preparato la camera per te.**

TRANSLATION 3

At the station

PETER Hello, Luisa, you've arrived at last!

LUISA Sorry, Peter, but the train was late when it left Siena [lit. "left late already from Siena"].

PETER It's all right. Are you tired now? What time did you leave home?

LUISA I left at six! First I went by bike to the station, and then I waited an hour for the train.

PETER Then let's go eat something right away. I've already booked the restaurant.

LUISA Great, thanks, Peter. Have you warned the landlady?

PETER Yes. She's already prepared the room for you.

3.5 PAST PARTICIPLES

Preparato, **venduto**, **finito** (prepared, sold, finished) are the past participles of **preparare**, **vendere**, and **finire**. They are formed by removing **-are**, **-ere**, **-ire** from the infinitive and adding **-ato**, **-uto**, **-ito**.

3.6 TALKING ABOUT THE PAST

To talk about a completed one-off event that occurred in the past, the present perfect tense is used in Italian. It is formed as follows:

3

1 For most verbs, by a conjugated form of the present tense of **avere** (to have) plus the past participle:

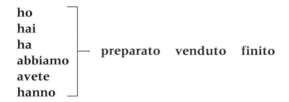

$$\left.\begin{array}{l} \textbf{ho} \\ \textbf{hai} \\ \textbf{ha} \\ \textbf{abbiamo} \\ \textbf{avete} \\ \textbf{hanno} \end{array}\right\} \quad \textbf{preparato} \quad \textbf{venduto} \quad \textbf{finito}$$

Examples:
Ieri Marco ha preparato il pranzo.
Yesterday Mark prepared lunch.
Ieri abbiamo venduto la casa.
Yesterday we sold the house.
Ieri ho finito alle 9.
Yesterday I finished at 9.

2 For certain verbs (intransitive verbs, or verbs that have no direct object), by using the present tense of **essere** (to be) plus the past participle. These include verbs of motion, such as "to go," "to arrive," "to leave," and of lack of motion, such as **stare***, **rimanere** (to stay, remain), etc.:

*Note that **stare** and **essere** are the same in the perfect tenses: **sono stato/a** (I have been/stayed), etc.

	andare (to go)		cadere (to fall)	
sono	andato,	andata	caduto,	caduta
sei	"	"	"	"
è	"	"	"	"
siamo	andati,	andate	caduti,	cadute
siete	"	"	"	"
sono	"	"	"	"

	partire (to leave)	
sono	partito,	partita
sei	"	"
è	"	"
siamo	partiti,	partite
siete	"	"
sono	"	"

Note that when the auxiliary verb is **essere**, the past participle must agree with the subject:

Maria è caduta. Maria (f.) has fallen/fell.
Marco è caduto. Marco (m.) has fallen/fell.
Gli studenti sono andati.
The students (m. pl.) have gone/went.
Le ragazze sono state qui.
The girls (f. pl.) have been/were here.

Exercise 7

Answer the following questions on Conversation 3:

1 Dove è andato Peter?
2 Perché è arrivata in ritardo Luisa?
3 Da dove è partita Luisa?
4 Che cosa ha prenotato Peter?
5 Che cosa ha preparato la padrona di casa?

Exercise 8

Change the following sentences using "ieri" (yesterday) and the present perfect tense to talk about the past:

Example:
Luisa arriva alle tre.→ Ieri Luisa è arrivata alle tre.

1 Mario arriva alle tre.
2 Il treno parte alle nove.
3 L'autobus arriva in ritardo.
4 Maria parte con il treno.
5 I signori Bianchi arrivano alle due.
6 Le valigie cadono per terra.
7 La passeggera va in macchina.
8 Noi (f.) partiamo all'una.
9 Voi (m.) andate in treno?
10 I viaggiatori vanno a prendere il taxi.

3

Exercise 9

Change these sentences using "un'ora fa" (an hour ago) and the present perfect tense:

Examples:
Preparo la camera.→ Un'ora fa ho preparato la camera.
Sentiamo la radio.→ Un'ora fa abbiamo sentito la radio.

1 Guido la macchina.
2 Mangio il pranzo.
3 Maria prepara la colazione.
4 Vendiamo la nostra macchina.
5 Comprano i biglietti.
6 I passeggeri guardano l'orario.
7 Senti questo rumore?
8 Finiamo il pranzo.
9 Prenotiamo il ristorante.
10 Portano le valigie sul treno.

Un viaggio d'affari

Francesca has just returned from a business trip to
Sardinia and tells her husband, Marino, what she has done
and seen there.

FRANCESCA	**Ciao Marino, finalmente sono arrivata.**
MARINO	**Ciao. Com'è andato il volo?**
FRANCESCA	**Bene. Ma l'aereo ha fatto scalo ad Alghero e il volo è durato tre ore.**
MARINO	**Sei stata sempre a Cagliari?**
FRANCESCA	**No, ho preso una macchina a noleggio e sono andata anche a Nuoro per due giorni.**
MARINO	**Ci sono stato anch'io. È bella vero?**
FRANCESCA	**Sì, molto. Ma non ho avuto molto tempo per vedere la città.**
MARINO	**Hai firmato quel famoso contratto per il nuovo albergo?**
FRANCESCA	**Sì, ho deciso di accettare la loro offerta. E ho anche visto il nuovo direttore.**
MARINO	**Bene. Hai fatto molto.**
FRANCESCA	**Eh sì, ma la prossima volta vorrei restare più a lungo. E tu, cos'hai fatto di bello?**
MARINO	**Anch'io ho lavorato molto. Ma vedi, ho anche preparato il tuo piatto preferito per stasera.**
FRANCESCA	**Fantastico! Sei stato bravo.**

A business trip

FRANCESCA	Hi, Marino, I've arrived at last.
MARINO	Hello. How was the flight?
FRANCESCA	Fine, but the plane stopped in Alghero, and the flight lasted three hours.
MARINO	Did you stay in Cagliari all the time?
FRANCESCA	No, I rented a car and went to Nuoro as well for two days.
MARINO	I've been there, too. It's beautiful, isn't it?
FRANCESCA	Yes, very. But I didn't have much time to see the town.
MARINO	Did you sign that famous contract for the new hotel?
FRANCESCA	Yes, I decided to accept their offer. I also saw the new manager.
MARINO	Good. You've done a lot.
FRANCESCA	Yes, but next time I'd like to stay longer. And what have you been doing?
MARINO	I've been working a lot, too. But look, I've also made your favorite dish for tonight.
FRANCESCA	Great! You've done well (lit. "have been good")!

3

3.7 IRREGULAR VERBS

Here are five key verbs with an irregular past participle (these are important to learn for the perfect tenses):

decidere:	**deciso**	**ho deciso**	I (have) decided
essere:	**stato**	**sono stato/a**	I was, have been
fare:	**fatto**	**ho fatto**	I did, have done
prendere:	**preso**	**ho preso**	I took, have taken
vedere:	**visto**	**ho visto**	I saw, have seen

And both key verbs below are irregular in the present tense:

fare (to do, make)   **andare** (to go)
faccio I do, make   **vado** I go
fai   **vai**
fa   **va**
facciamo   **andiamo**
fate   **andate**
fanno   **vanno**

Exercise 10

You have just arrived from Sardinia, and your host (O) asks you about your trip. Complete the dialogue using the clues given:

o Buongiorno signor Taylor, ben arrivato. Com'è andato il viaggio?

YOU (Very well, thank you. But my plane left late from Rome. So I arrived late in Cagliari.)

o A che ora è partito da Roma?

YOU (At 10:45, but I left home at seven o'clock.)

o Ha preso il taxi dall'aeroporto?

YOU (No, I rented a car.)

o C'è sempre molto traffico, vero?

YOU (Yes, but I decided to rent the car for one week.)

o È un'ottima idea, così è più facile visitare la città e i dintorni.

YOU (I have not seen the center. I would like to go to all the famous places.)

Exercise 11

Rewrite Conversation 4 as a report of what Francesca did in Sardinia, beginning with "Oggi Francesca è tornata...."

Try to remember these key phrases related to the grammar and topics of this week:

Quel ragazzo ha preso l'autobus.
A che ora parte il treno?
Parte alle diciannove.
Ieri sono andata in Sardegna.

3

The words listed below have all appeared this week. Check how well you remember them by covering up one column or the other and translating them.

aereo (m.) [ah-<u>eh</u>-rreh-oh]	airplane
aeroporto (m.) [ah-eh-rroh-pohr-toh]	airport
affari (m. pl.) [af-fah-rree]	business
affollato [af-fohl-lah-toh]	crowded
albergo (m.) [ahl-behr-goh]	hotel
andare [ahn-dah-rreh]	to go
andata e ritorno (biglietto di) [ahn-dah-tah eh rree-tohr-noh]	return (ticket)
appuntamento (m.) [ahp-poon-tah-men-toh]	appointment, meeting
arrivare [ahr-ree-vah-rreh]	to arrive
aspettare [ahs-peht-tah-rreh]	to wait for
autobus (m.) [<u>ow</u>-toh-boos]	bus
automobile (f.) [ow-toh-m<u>oh</u>-bee-leh]	car
autostrada (f.) [ow-toh-strah-dah]	motorway
avvisare [ahv-vee-zah-rreh]	to warn
bicicletta (f.) [bee-chee-kleht-tah]	bicycle
biglietto (m.) [bee-l'yeht-toh]	ticket
bravo [brah-voh]	good, clever
cadere [kah-deh-rreh]	to fall
Cagliari (f.) [k<u>ah</u>-l'yah-rree]	Cagliari
cambiare [kahm-byah-rreh]	to change
caro [kah-rroh]	expensive

cartina, carta (f.) [kahr-tee-nah, kahr-tah]	map
chiesa (f.) [kieh-zah]	church
città (f.) [cheet-t<u>ah</u>]	town, city
ci vuole [chee-vwoh-leh]	it takes
comprare [kom-prah-rreh]	to buy
con [kon]	with
contratto (m.) [kon-traht-toh]	contract
corso (m.) [kohr-soh]	road, main street
costare [kos-tah-rreh]	to cost
decidere [deh-ch<u>ee</u>-deh-rreh]	to decide
di più [dee py<u>oo</u>]	more
direttore / direttrice [dee-rreht-toh-rreh/tree-cheh]	director
diritto [dee-rreet-toh]	straight
distanza (f.) [dees-tahn-tzah]	distance
dunque [doon-qweh]	so, then
durata (f.) [doo-rrah-tah]	duration
eccola [<u>eh</u>k-koh-lah]	here she/it (f.) is
facile [f<u>ah</u>-chee-leh]	easy, simple
fantastico [fahn-t<u>ah</u>s-tee-koh]	fantastic
fare [fah-rreh]	to do, to make
fermata (f.) [fehr-mah-tah]	stop
ferrovia (f.) [fehr-roh-v<u>ee</u>-ah]	railroad
finalmente [fee-nahl-mehn-teh]	at last
finire [fee-nee-rreh]	to finish
fino a [fee-noh ah]	until
giornalaio (m.) [johr-nah-lay-oh]	newsagent
giusto [joos-toh]	right
gomma (f.) [gohm-mah]	tyre
gratis [grah-tees]	free
guasto [gwahs-toh]	broken down
guidare [gwee-dah-rreh]	to drive
idea (f.) [ee-deh-ah]	idea
imparare [im-pah-rrah-rreh]	to learn
informazione (f.) [in-fohr-mah-dzioh-neh]	information
in orario [in oh-rrah-rrioh]	on time
in ritardo [in rree-tahr-doh]	late
istituto (m.) [is-tee-too-toh]	institute, faculty
lezione (f.) [leh-dzioh-neh]	lesson

mezzanotte (f.) [mehdz-zah-noht-teh]	midnight
mezzo [mehdz-zoh]	half
mezzogiorno (m.) [mehdz-zoh-johr-noh]	midday
mille grazie [meel-leh grah-tzieh]	many thanks
minuto (m.) [mee-noo-toh]	minute
motocicletta (f.) [moh-toh-chee-kleht-tah]	motorcycle
museo (m.) [moo-zeh-oh]	museum
noleggio (m.) [noh-lehj-joh]	rental, hire
obbligatorio [ohb-blee-gah-toh-rrioh]	compulsory
offerta (f.) [ohf-fehr-tah]	offer
ogni [oh-n'yee]	every
ora (f.) [oh-rrah]	hour, time (of the day)
orario (m.) [oh-rrah-rrioh]	timetable
padrone/a [pah-droh-neh/nah]	landlord/lady
partire [pahr-tee-rreh]	to leave
passare [pahs-sah-rreh]	to pass, spend, go by
passeggero/a [pahs-sehj-jeh-rroh/rrah]	passenger
per terra [pehr tehr-rah]	on the floor
perché [pehr-keh]	why, because
piatto (m.) [piaht-toh]	dish, plate
più a lungo [pyoo ah loon-goh]	longer (time)
poi [poy]	then
politecnico (m.) [poh-lee-tehk-nee-koh]	polytechnic
portare [pohr-tah-rreh]	to carry
posto (m.) [pohs-toh]	seat, place
pranzo (m.) [prahn-tzoh]	lunch
preferito [preh-feh-rree-toh]	favorite
prenotare [preh-noh-tah-rreh]	to book, to reserve
preparare [preh-pah-rrah-rreh]	to prepare
proprio [proh-prioh]	really, quite
qual, quale [kwahl, kwah-leh]	which
qualche [kwal-keh]	some
qualcosa [kwahl-koh-zah]	something
qualsiasi [kwahl-see-ah-see]	whatever, any
qualunque [kwahl-oon-kweh]	whatever, any

3

quando [kwahn-doh]	when
radio (f.) [rrah-dioh]	radio
riservato [rree-zehr-vah-toh]	reserved, booked
ritardo (m.) [rree-tahr-doh]	delay
ritornare/tornare [rree-tohr-nah-rreh]	to go/come back, return
salire [sah-lee-rreh]	to climb, to go up
scendere [sh<u>eh</u>n-deh-rreh]	to go down, to descend
scompartimento (m.) [skohm-pahr-tee-mehn-toh]	compartment
seduto [seh-doo-toh]	seated
semaforo (m.) [seh-**m**ah-foh-rroh]	traffic light
sempre [sehm-preh]	always
sgonfio [zgohn-fioh]	flat (tire)
sicuro [see-koo-rroh]	sure
soggiorno (m.) [sohj-johr-noh]	stay
sportello (m.) [spohr-tehl-loh]	door (of car, train)
stanco [stahn-koh]	tired
stasera [stah-seh-rrah]	tonight
studiare [stoo-diah-rreh]	to study
tabaccaio (m.) [tah-bahk-kay-oh]	tobacconist
taxi (m.) [tahk-see]	taxi
traffico (m.) [tr<u>ah</u>f-fee-koh]	traffic
treno (m.) [treh-noh]	train
ufficio informazioni (m.) [oof-fee-choh in-fohr-mah-dzioh-nee]	inquiry desk
università (f.) [oo-nee-vehr-see-t<u>ah</u>]	university
vagone (m.) [vah-goh-neh]	carriage
valido [v<u>ah</u>-lee-doh]	valid
veloce [veh-loh-cheh]	fast
vendere [v<u>eh</u>n-deh-rreh]	to sell
veramente [veh-rrah-mehn-teh]	really
vettura (f.) [veht-too-rrah]	carriage
via (f.) [vee-ah]	street
volo (m.) [voh-loh]	flight
volta (f.) [vohl-tah]	time (occasion)
vorrei [vohr-reh-ee]	I would like

Week 4

You will learn to:
- book a room
- talk about buying property
- ask about facilities at a campsite

The grammar includes:
- modal verbs ("want," "must," "can")
- verbs ending in **-isco** in the first person: **finire**, **pulire**, **capire**
- the imperative
- irregular verbs: **venire** ("to come"), **tenere** ("to keep," "to hold"), **dare** ("to give"), **stare** ("to stay")
- numbers from 1,000 to 1,000,000,000
- dates, years, months, days of the week

4

CONVERSATION 1

All'agenzia di soggiorno, Lago di Garda

Rita is on vacation at Lake Garda and is looking for cheap accommodations. At the local tourist office, she talks to Gianni:

GIANNI **Buongiorno signora, desidera?**

RITA **Vorrei restare a Garda per due settimane. Ci sono pensioni non troppo care?**

GIANNI **La pensione completa costa novanta euro al giorno come minimo.**

RITA **Preferisco qualcosa di meno caro.**

GIANNI **Può andare in campeggio: quindici euro per notte più l'affitto della tenda.**

RITA **Ci sono anche camere in case private?**

GIANNI **Certo, ma deve fissare il prezzo con la padrona. Vuole guardare la lista?**

RITA **Grazie, volentieri. E qual è il prezzo di solito?**

GIANNI **Dai venticinque ai trentacinque euro per notte.**

RITA **Così è meglio per me. Grazie della lista. Arrivederci.**

At the tourist office, Lake Garda

GIANNI Good morning, may I help you?

RITA I would like to stay in Garda for two weeks. Are there any guesthouses that aren't too expensive?

GIANNI Full board is 90 euros a day minimum.

RITA I'd prefer something cheaper.

GIANNI You can go to a campsite: 15 euros a day, plus the rent of the tent.

RITA Are there rooms in private houses as well?

GIANNI Yes, but you have to arrange the price with the landlady. Do you want to see the list?

RITA Yes, gladly. What's the price usually?

GIANNI From 25 to 35 euros a night.

RITA That's better for me. Thank you for the list. Goodbye.

4.1 MODAL VERBS: WANT, CAN, MUST

The equivalent of the modal verb "want" is **volere**, "can" is **potere**, and "must" is **dovere**. As in English, Italian modal verbs are conjugated and the main verb is in the infinitive:

vuoi guardare	you (fam.) want to look at
puoi andare	you (fam.) can go
devi fissare	you (fam.) must arrange

Note that these verbs are irregular in the present tense:

volere	**potere**	**dovere**
voglio (I want)	**posso** (I can)	**devo** (I must)
vuoi	**puoi**	**devi**
vuole	**può**	**deve**
vogliamo	**possiamo**	**dobbiamo**
volete	**potete**	**dovete**
vogliono	**possono**	**devono**

Note also that, as in English, when saying what you want, it is more polite to use **vorrei** ("I would like"):

vorrei restare   I would like to stay

(This is the conditional; for more about the conditional, see section 5.2.)

Exercise 1

Translate into Italian:

1 Rita wants to rent an apartment.
2 Can't I look at this list?
3 I would like to book a room.
4 We cannot pay much.
5 We must leave at 9:00.
6 Do you (pl.) want to go to the campsite?
7 They can come today.
8 He must pay more.
9 Do you (formal) want to stay in a boarding house?
10 If I can, I want to stay in Venice for three days.

4.2 VERBS WITH -ISC- CONJUGATIONS

There is a group of **-ire** verbs that form the present tense conjugations by adding **-isc-** in front of most of the endings. For example:

finire (to finish)

finisco (I finish)
finisci
finisce
finiamo
finite
finiscono

Other verbs like **finire** are:

preferire	>	**preferisco**	I prefer
pulire	>	**pulisco**	I clean
capire	>	**capisco**	I understand

Exercise 2

Answer the following questions addressed to "you" in the familiar, using "voglio," "posso," or "devo" plus the infinitive and the given phrase:

Example:
Quando devi partire? ... adesso
Devo partire adesso.

Quando vuoi andare? ... all'una
Voglio andare all'una.

1 Quando devi andare? ... più tardi

2 Dove devi aspettare? ... alla stazione

3 Chi devi vedere? ... la mia padrona di casa

4 Quando vuoi venire? ... alle tre

5 Dove vuoi restare? ... in albergo

6 Chi vuoi vedere? ... i miei amici

7 Quando puoi venire? ... a mezzogiorno

8 Dove puoi restare? ... al campeggio

9 Chi puoi invitare? ... una collega

10 Quando puoi pagare? ... stasera

4

All'agenzia immobiliare

Hugh O'Sullivan wants to buy a small house in Umbria
and is looking at various properties with signora Dossi,
the estate agent:

DOSSI **Ho preparato una lista di varie proprietà
come vuole Lei.**

HUGH **Guardi, io non posso spendere più di
settantacinquemila dollari.**

DOSSI **Cioè più o meno settantacinquemila euro.
Per quel prezzo abbiamo appartamenti
non restaurati a Gubbio e anche qualche
casetta fuori.**

HUGH **Vorrei una casetta in campagna, ma le case
quanto costano?**

DOSSI **Ci sono rustici per ottantamila euro, ma
devono essere rimodernati.**

HUGH **Capisco, ma ci sono l'acqua e la luce
elettrica?**

DOSSI **Sì. Prenda questi fogli con le fotografie e
tutti i particolari delle case. Controlli dove
sono sulla piantina e vada pure a vedere dal
di fuori.**

HUGH **Ottima idea. E se voglio visitare l'interno,
telefono.**

DOSSI **Ma se vuole vedere diverse case, telefoni al
mattino, così ho più tempo.**

4

At the estate agent's

DOSSI I have prepared a list of various properties as you requested.

HUGH But you see, I cannot spend more than 75,000 dollars.

DOSSI That is more or less 75,000 euros. For that price we have apartments that need restoring in Gubbio and also some small houses on the outskirts.

HUGH I'd like a small country house, but how much are they?

DOSSI There are farmhouses for 80,000 euros, but they need modernizing.

HUGH I see, but is there water and electricity (literally "electric lighting")?

DOSSI Yes. Take these information sheets with the photos and all the details about the houses. Check where they are on the map, and do go and see them from the outside.

HUGH Excellent idea. And if I want to see the inside, I will call.

DOSSI But if you want to see several houses, call in the morning when I have more time.

4

Exercise 3

Read and listen to the conversation, then answer the following questions:

1 Che tipo di proprietà vuole il signor O'Sullivan?

2 Dove preferisce abitare?

3 Può trovare un appartamento a Gubbio per settantacinquemila euro?

4 Il signor O'Sullivan può visitare l'interno delle case?

5 C'è l'acqua in questi rustici?

4.3 THE IMPERATIVE

To ask or tell someone to do something, the imperative (or command form) is used. Here are the familiar, formal, and plural forms of the imperative:

parlare	prendere	sentire	finire
(tu) parla!	prendi!	senti!	finisci!
(Lei) parli!	prenda!	senta!	finisca!
(noi) parliamo!	prendiamo!	sentiamo!	finiamo!
(voi) parlate!	prendete!	sentite!	finite!

Examples:
Carlo, parla piano!
Speak slowly, Carlo! (fam.)
Signora Rossi, prenda questo posto.
Take this seat, Ms. Rossi. (form.)
Ragazzi, finite il compito.
Finish your homework, boys.
Entrate, signore e signori!
Come in, ladies and gentlemen!
Parliamo italiano.
Let's speak in Italian.

NOTE: If you want to ask a favor, you use **un po'** or **per favore**, and if you want to encourage or allow someone to do something, you use **pure** after the imperative.

Posso sedermi? Certo, si sieda pure!
May I sit down? Sure, have a seat!
Ragazzi, venite un po' qui!
Guys, come over here!

However, it is not impolite to use the imperative even without any of these expressions in Italian. A particularly polite way of attracting someone's attention is to use **senta** (literally this means "hear!"):

to a stranger: **Senta, signora, sa dov'è la stazione?**
to a friend: **Senti, cosa fai oggi?**

Exercise 4

Reply using the formal form of the imperative.

Example:

Scusi, devo provare?→ Sì, provi pure!

1 Scusi, devo scrivere?

2 Scusi, devo cominciare?

3 Scusi, devo finire?

4 Scusi, devo mangiare?

5 Scusi, devo pulire?

6 Scusi, devo chiudere?

7 Scusi, devo servire?

8 Scusi, devo guardare?

9 Scusi, devo partire?

10 Scusi, devo entrare?

Exercise 5

Reply as in Exercise 4, but this time use the familiar form of the imperative.

Example:

Scusa, devo provare?→ Sì, prova pure!

Exercise 6

Now change the questions and answers in Exercise 4 to the plural (asking if "we" can do something and answering that "you" [pl.] certainly can).

Example:

Scusate, dobbiamo provare?→ Sì, provate pure!

4.4 NEGATIVE IMPERATIVE

To tell people what <u>not</u> to do, you put **non** in front of the imperative in the formal or plural forms:

Non entri! Do not enter!
Non entrate!
Non entriamo!

BUT in the familiar form, you use **non** and the infinitive:

Carlo, entra! *but* **Carlo, non entrare!**

Exercise 7

Change all these imperatives into the negative.
Example:
Maria, apri la porta!→ Maria, non aprire la porta!
Signora, apra la porta!→ Signora, non apra la porta!

1 Signora, chiuda la finestra, per favore!
2 Mario, porta la mia valigia, per favore!
3 Piero, guarda la televisione, per favore!
4 Signora, prenda la chiave, per favore!
5 Maria, prendi la chiave, per favore!
6 Ragazzi, guardate questo salotto, per favore!
7 Ragazze, prendete questa strada, per favore!
8 Signor Rossi, guardi là per favore!
9 Scendiamo insieme le scale!
10 Sandro, prendi l'ombrello!

4.5 IRREGULAR PRESENT-TENSE VERBS

venire (to come)	tenere (to keep)	dare (to give)	stare (to stay)
vengo	tengo	do	sto
vieni	tieni	dai	stai
viene	tiene	dà	sta
veniamo	teniamo	diamo	stiamo
venite	tenete	date	state
vengono	tengono	danno	stanno

Note that **stare** is used in many idiomatic expressions in Italian that in English would require a variety of other verbs.

Examples:
Come sta?
How are you?
stare tranquillo/calmo/fermo
to keep quiet/calm/still
stare bene/male
to feel well/unwell
stare attento
to pay attention

4.6 IRREGULAR IMPERATIVES

Note that the **Lei** form of the imperative is obtained from the stem of the first-person singular of the present tense (this applies to both regular and irregular verbs):

	present	imperative
parlare	parlo	parli
sentire	sento	senta
venire	vengo	venga
tenere	tengo	tenga
andare	vado	vada
fare	faccio	faccia

BUT the following verbs have irregular imperatives:

	essere	avere	dare	stare
(tu)	sii	abbi	da' / dai	sta' / stai
(Lei)	sia	abbia	dia	stia
(noi)	siamo	abbiamo	diamo	stiamo
(voi)	siate	abbiate	date	state

Examples:

Sta' fermo!
Keep still!
Sia paziente!
Be patient!
Stia calma!
Keep calm!
Non abbia paura!
Don't be afraid!
Dia una bella mancia!
Give a good tip!
Siate gentili!
Be kind!

4

Exercise 8

Answer the following questions using the formal imperative as in the example:

Question: Vengo anch'io?
Answer: Sì, certo, venga pure.

1 Vado anch'io?

2 Sto qui anch'io?

3 Faccio io?

4 Do anch'io i soldi?

5 Tengo il resto?

6 Vengo anch'io?

7 Finisco io?

8 Pulisco anche la cucina?

9 Bevo anch'io il vino?

10 Leggo anch'io la lista?

4.7 THE EURO AND MORE NUMBERS: 1,000 TO 1,000,000,000

THE EURO
Even when used with amounts of more than one, **euro** is always singular. It is divided into 100 **centesimi**.

Questa rivista costa cinque euro e cinquanta (centesimi).
This magazine costs €5.50.

MORE NUMBERS
In Italian, a written number has a period separating every thousand or multiple of a thousand:

1.000	**mille**
1.350	**milletrecentocinquanta**
2.000	**duemila**
3.000	**tremila**
100.000	**centomila**
1.000.000	**un milione**
1.000.000.000	**un miliardo/un bilione**

Note: **mille** becomes **-mila** in the plural.

4.8 DAYS OF THE WEEK, MONTHS, AND DATES

Giorni della settimana   Days of the week

lunedì	Monday
martedì	Tuesday
mercoledì	Wednesday
giovedì	Thursday
venerdì	Friday
sabato	Saturday
domenica	Sunday

Mesi	Months
gennaio	January
febbraio	February
marzo	March
aprile	April
maggio	May
giugno	June
luglio	July
agosto	August
settembre	September
ottobre	October
novembre	November
dicembre	December

Note that days and months are written without a capital letter in Italian.

DATES

When giving the date in Italian, you use cardinal numbers (i.e., "two," "three," "four," etc., not "second," "third," "fourth"), followed by the month and the year.

The year is read like any other number. For example, a year such as 1500 will be read as "one thousand five hundred" and not as "fifteen hundred."

2 December 2021   **2 dicembre 2021
(il due dicembre duemilaventuno)**

BUT you use **primo** (first), for the first day of the month:

1st July 2022   **1 luglio 2022
(il primo luglio duemilaventidue)**

When mentioning the year, you use **nel**:

in 1900   **nel 1900 (nel millenovecento)**

Exercise 9

Answer the following questions as in the example:

Example:

Che giorno è oggi? ... Wednesday.→ Oggi è mercoledì.

1	Che giorno è oggi?	... Tuesday
2	Qual è la data?	... 31st January 2021
3	Quanto costa la Sua casa?	... €300,000
4	Qual è il mese?	... August
5	Quanto costano le cartoline?	... €1
6	Quanti abitanti ha Verona?	... 600,000
7	Quando è finita la guerra?	... in 1945
8	Quando è nata (was born) Sofia Loren?	... in 1932
9	Quanto costa il biglietto?	... €6.65
10	Quanto costa l'aereo per Milano?	... €120

CONVERSATION 3

Al campeggio

Tony and his friend have arrived at the Campeggio Miramare and talk to the owner, signora Calvi:

TONY **Senta signora, c'è posto per la nostra roulotte qui?**

CALVI **Avete prenotato?**

TONY **No, mi dispiace.**

CALVI **Beh, vediamo. Per quanti giorni e per quante persone?**

TONY **Siamo in due, e vorremmo restare almeno una settimana.**

CALVI **Per una settimana, fino al 6 agosto, va bene.**

TONY **Possiamo vedere prima il posto?**

CALVI	**Certo. Andiamo! Vedete, queste sono le docce, qui c'è la cucina e la lavanderia e questi sono i gabinetti.**
TONY	**Scusi, non capisco, che cos'è la lavanderia?**
CALVI	**È il posto dove può lavare la Sua roba.**
TONY	**Ah, ho capito! E dove possiamo fare la spesa?**
CALVI	**Qui al campeggio c'è un supermercato e a Garda ci sono tutti i negozi.**
TONY	**Benissimo. Allora lo prendiamo.**

TRANSLATION 3

At the campsite

TONY	Excuse me, is there a place for our caravan here?
CALVI	Have you booked?
TONY	No, sorry.
CALVI	Well, let's see. For how many days and for how many people?
TONY	There are two of us (lit. "We are two"), and we'd like to stay at least a week.
CALVI	For one week, until August 6; that's fine.
TONY	Can we see the pitch first?
CALVI	Certainly. Let's go. Look (lit. "see"), these are the showers, here is the kitchen and the launderette, and these are the toilets.
TONY	Excuse me, I don't understand ... what is a "launderette"?
CALVI	It's the place where you can wash your clothes.
TONY	Ah, got it! Where can we do the shopping?
CALVI	There is a supermarket here on the site, and in Garda you'll find (lit. "there are") all the shops.
TONY	Excellent. Then we'll take it.

Exercise 10

Read and listen to Conversation 3, checking any new expressions, then try to answer these questions without looking at the text:

1 Che servizi ci sono al campeggio?
2 Tony e il suo amico hanno la tenda?
3 Hanno prenotato il posto prima?
4 Possono fare la spesa al campeggio?

Exercise 11

Translate the following sentences:

1 They must book the room before August.
2 They didn't go to ("in") Italy in 2021.
3 We prefer an apartment on the ground floor.
4 They want to buy a house in the country.
5 Can we look at the farmhouse next week?
6 The appointment is for next Friday at 3 p.m.
7 The estate agent can arrange a visit in the morning.
8 I would like to come, but today I have to stay at home.
9 I'm sorry, but I want a room with a bathroom.
10 Don't buy (formal) this house, it is too far from the center.

Vorrei venire ma non posso.
Signora, guardi un po' questo appartamento!
Il 6 agosto tutti devono partire.
Tenga pure il resto!

You may have noticed that we're no longer including the phonetic transcriptions, as you should be getting more familiar with the pronunciation, but keep listening to the audio!

acqua (f.)	water
affittare	to rent
affitto (m.)	rental
anno (m.)	year
avere paura	to be afraid
balcone (m.)	balcony
campeggio (m.)	campsite
capire	to understand
caro	expensive
casetta (f.)	small house, cottage
centesimo (m.)	cent
chiudere	to close
cioè	that is, i.e.
compito (m.)	homework
dare	to give
data (f.)	date
di fuori/fuori	outside
diverso	different
diversi (pl.)	several
doccia (f.)	shower
dovere	to have to, must
fissare	to arrange
foglio (m.)	sheet of paper
fumare	to smoke
gabinetto (m.)	lavatory, toilet
guardare	to look at
interno (m.)	interior
lavanderia (f.)	launderette, laundry area
lista (f.)	list
luce (f.)	light

4

mancia (f.)	tip (gratuity)
mattino (m.)	morning
meno	less
mi dispiace	I'm sorry
minimo (m.)	minimum
nato/a	born (past participle of **nascere**)
notte (f.)	night
oggi	today
paziente	patient
pensione completa (f.)	full board
piano	slowly
piantina (f.)	map
preferire	to prefer
prezzo (m.)	price
pulire	to clean
restaurare	to restore
rimodernare	to modernize
roulotte *(f.)*	caravan
rustico (m.)	farmhouse
salotto (m.)	lounge, living room
scale (f. pl.)	stairs
scendere	to go down
sedersi	to sit down
servire	to serve
servizi (m. pl.)	facilities
settimana (f.)	week
spesa (f.)	shopping
stare	to stay, to be
stare attento	to pay attention, to be careful
stare calmo	to keep calm
tardi	late
tassa di soggiorno *(f.)*	tourist tax
tenda (f.)	tent
tenere	to keep, to hold
troppo	too, too much
venire	to come
volentieri	willingly, gladly
volere	to want, to wish
vorremmo	we would like (conditional of **volere**)

Week 5

You will learn:
- how to order a drink and a meal
- to accept or refuse offers of drinks or food
- to invite others for drinks and meals

The grammar will include:
- personal object pronouns ("me," "you," "him," "her," "us," etc.)
- the conditional ("would")
- imperatives with pronouns
- irregular verbs: **bere, cuocere, dire, sapere**
- two ways to express "can": **sapere** and **potere**
- likes and dislikes: **mi piace/non mi piace**
- uses of the preposition **da**

CONVERSATION 1

Al bar dell'albergo

5

Bill White is having a drink at the bar with Nina Fazzini, another guest at the hotel.

BILL **Che cosa prende da bere?**
NINA **Io prenderei un aperitivo analcolico, e Lei?**
BILL **Io prendo un martini.**
NINA **Se permette, oggi offro io.**
BILL **Ma no, mi ha già invitato ieri.**
NINA **Si figuri. Il Martini, lo preferisce secco o rosso?**
BILL **Rosso, grazie.**
NINA **Eccoli. Salute!**
BILL **Salute! Allora Le posso offrire una tartina?**
NINA **Grazie, la prendo proprio volentieri.**
BILL **Sì, le fanno buone, qui.**
NINA **È la loro specialità.**
BILL **Ne prendiamo un'altra?**
NINA **Sì grazie. E un altro aperitivo?**

At the hotel bar

BILL What would you like (lit. "you take") to drink?
NINA I'll have (lit. "would take") a nonalcoholic aperitif, and you?
BILL I'll have (lit. "I take") a martini.
NINA Allow me, today I'll pay (lit. "I offer").
BILL Thank you, but you treated me yesterday.
NINA Don't mention it. Do you prefer your martini dry or sweet (lit. "red")?
BILL Sweet, please.
NINA Here they are. Cheers!
BILL Cheers! May I offer you a canapé?
NINA Thank you, I'd love to try one.
BILL Yes, they make good canapés here.
NINA It's their specialty.
BILL Shall we have another?
NINA Yes, please. And another aperitif?

Exercise 1

Read through section 5.1, and then answer these questions about Conversation 1 using "lo," "la," or "le" followed by the verb.

Example:
La signora Fazzini prende un Martini?→ No, non lo prende.

1 Il signor White prende un aperitivo analcolico?
2 Chi offre l'aperitivo?
3 Chi offre la tartina?
4 Il signor White prende un Martini?
5 Nina e Bill mangiano le tartine?

5.1 OBJECT PRONOUNS: ME, YOU, HIM, ETC.

Object pronouns, both direct (me, him, etc.) and indirect (to me, to him, etc.), are used more often in Italian than in English, so it's important to learn to recognize them. The more you use them, the more familiar they'll become.

Take, for example, the question, "Do you know this lady?" In English, you'd reply, "Yes, I do," or "No, I don't." But the modal verb "do" does not exist in Italian, so the polite way to answer would be to repeat the verb, using the relevant pronoun to refer to the person:

Conosce la signora? **No, non la conosco.**
Sì, la conosco.

These pronouns in Italian are placed <u>before</u> the verb, except with an infinitive and some forms of the imperative, as we'll see later in this week's lesson.

To the English ear, it may sound impolite to use personal object pronouns as in the example above, but this is not the case in Italian.

direct object pronouns		indirect object pronouns	
me	**mi**	**mi**	to me
you (fam.)	**ti**	**ti**	to you (fam.)
him, it (m.)	**lo**	**gli**	to him
her, it (f.)	**la**	**le**	to her
you (form.)	**La***	**Le***	to you (form.)
us	**ci**	**ci**	to us
you (pl.)	**vi**	**vi**	to you (pl.)
them (m.)	**li**	**gli/(loro)***	to them
them (f.)	**le**		

* As with **Lei, Suo, Sua**, etc., it is customary to use a capital letter for **La** and **Le** in the formal.

** Note that the indirect object pronoun **gli** has now taken the place of **loro** in everyday speech.

Note that **mi** and **ti**, **ci** and **vi** are used as both direct and indirect object pronouns:

he sees me	**mi vede**
and	
he speaks to me	**mi parla**

he sees you (pl.)	**vi vede**
and	
he speaks to you (pl.)	**vi parla**

BUT in the third person, there are different pronouns:

he sees him	**lo vede**
but	
he speaks to him	**gli parla**

he sees her	**la vede**
but	
he speaks to her	**le parla**

he sees you	**La vede**
but	
he speaks to you	**Le parla**

he sees them (m.)	**li vede**
he sees them (f.)	**le vede**
but	
he speaks to them (m. & f.)	**gli parla (parla loro)**

Exercise 2

Answer these questions using the direct object pronouns "lo," "la," "li," "le":

Examples:

Prendi spesso l'aperitivo?→ Sì, lo prendo spesso.

Bevi spesso la birra?→ Sì, la bevo spesso.

1 Guardi spesso la televisione?

2 Compri spesso le patate?

3 Inviti spesso i tuoi amici?

4 Bevi spesso il caffè?

5 Prendi spesso il treno?

6 Porti spesso la cravatta?

7 Mangi spesso le tartine?

8 Bevi spesso vini francesi?

9 Non bevi vini italiani?

10 Inviti spesso la tua vicina?

5

Exercise 3

Answer these questions using the indirect object pronouns "gli," "le":

Examples:

Quando parla a Maria?→ Le parlo adesso.

Quando parla a Giovanni?→ Gli parlo adesso.

1 Quando parla a Sua moglie?

2 Quando parla al direttore?

3 Quando telefona a Giuseppe?

4 Quando risponde a Laura?

5 Quando scrive agli studenti?

6 Quando scrive alle ragazze?

7 Quando risponde a Giuseppe e Maria?

8 Quando telefona al padrone di casa?

9 Quando parla ai signori Bianchi?

10 Quando scrive alla signora Rossi?

Exercise 4

Replace the words in bold with suitable direct or indirect object pronouns:

Example:
Il padre guarda **la televisione**.→ Il padre *la* guarda.
Non parlo **a Giovanni**.→ Non *gli* parlo.

1 Anna dà il numero **a Maria**.
2 Non sento **il rumore**.
3 Il signor Forti legge **la lista**.
4 La signora prende **le olive**.
5 Compriamo **i biglietti** qui.
6 Offro l'aperitivo **ai signori Danzi**.
7 Telefono **al mio ragazzo**.
8 Scrivete **a vostra madre**?
9 Che cosa portate **a vostro fratello**?
10 Il signor Rossi non lascia **la mancia**.

CONVERSATION 2

In osteria

Tony and his friend Jeff have been invited by some Italian people to join them at their local bar. Tony talks to Maria, one member of the group.

MARIA **Allora Tony cosa prendi?**
TONY **Io vorrei un espresso e Jeff dice che lascia fare a te.**
MARIA **Guarda che questa è un'osteria, dove si beve soprattutto vino. Non è un posto per turisti!**
TONY **Benissimo, allora un bicchiere di bianco per Jeff e un caffè per me, se fanno il caffè.**
MARIA **Sì, sì il caffè c'è, ma perché non lo prendi anche tu corretto, come me?**

TONY	Perché no, ma permettimi di pagare, oggi.
MARIA	Ma no, figurati!
TONY	No, no, insisto, oggi tocca a me!
MARIA	Come vuoi, e grazie. Salute!
TONY	Salute!

TRANSLATION 2

At the bar

MARIA	So what are you having, Tony?
TONY	I'd like an espresso, and Jeff says that he'll let you decide for him.
MARIA	This is [like] a bar, mind you, where people drink mainly wine. It's not a tourist place.
TONY	Fine, then a glass of white wine for Jeff and a coffee for me, if they do coffee.
MARIA	Yes, there is coffee, but why don't you have it with a shot of spirits, like me?
TONY	Why not, but let me pay today.
MARIA	No, no, no problem!
TONY	No, I insist, today it's my turn.
MARIA	As you wish, thank you. Cheers!
TONY	Cheers!

5

Exercise 5

Read the conversation, checking any new expressions, then answer these questions:

1 Che cosa beve Maria?

2 Tony beve il vino?

3 Che cos'è un'osteria?

4 Chi offre da bere oggi?

5 Chi beve vino bianco?

5.2 THE CONDITIONAL ("WOULD")

In Italian, as in English, the conditional is used to express the consequence of an imagined event: "would." It is formed by adding the following endings to the infinitive:

-i
-sti
-bbe
-mmo
-ste
-bbero

Note that in **-are** verbs, the **-a** changes to **-e**:

parlare	prendere	dormire
parlerei	prenderei	dormirei
parleresti	prenderesti	dormiresti
parlerebbe	prenderebbe	dormirebbe
parleremmo	prenderemmo	dormiremmo
parlereste	prendereste	dormireste
parlerebbero	prenderebbero	dormirebbero

Note also that the endings of the conditional are always regular, but the stem of some irregular verbs contracts:

avere:	avrei	I would have
essere:	sarei	I would be
vedere:	vedrei	I would see
venire:	verrei	I would come
volere:	vorrei	I would want
dovere:	dovrei	I would have to
potere:	potrei	I would be able to
bere:	berrei	I would drink
tenere:	terrei	I would keep/hold
andare:	andrei	I would go

Examples:

Verrei volentieri.
I would come with pleasure.
Potrebbero stare qui.
They could stay here.
Andresti da solo?
Would you go alone?

Exercise 6

Answer the following questions addressed to you, changing the present tense to the conditional and using the given phrase.

Examples:
Volete andare in treno?→ Sì, … ma costa troppo.
Sì, vorremmo andare ma costa troppo.
Vuoi andare in treno?→ Sì, … ma costa troppo.
Sì, vorrei andare ma costa troppo.

1 Dovete partire oggi? Sì, … ma abbiamo cambiato idea.

2 Devi andare a vedere la casa? Sì, … ma non ho la macchina.

3 Puoi venire oggi? Si, … ma più tardi.

4 Potete accompagnarlo? Sì, … in macchina.

5 Vuoi telefonare? Sì, … ma non ho il tempo.

6 Volete viaggiare in aereo? Sì, … ma non da soli.

7 Vuoi un aperitivo? No, … un cappuccino.

8 Volete mangiare adesso? No, … alle due.

9 Puoi venire in macchina? No, … in bicicletta.

10 Dovete restare in albergo? Sì, … per la cena.

Direct and indirect object pronouns always come after the imperative, the infinitive, and the term **ecco** and are attached to them to form one word. This doesn't change the word stress. The infinitive loses its final **e**:

Permettetemi!
Allow me! (pl.)
Prendilo!
Take it! (fam.)
Non prenderlo!
Don't take it! (fam.)
Potete accompagnarlo?
Can you accompany him? (pl.)
Eccoli ...
Here they are ...
Dimmi la verità.
Tell me the truth. (fam.)

Note that in the formal imperative, the object pronouns are placed <u>before</u> the verb:

Mi scusi!
Excuse me! (formal)
Non lo prenda!
Don't take it! (formal)

This is because the **Lei** form of the imperative is in fact borrowed from the present subjunctive. And you'll remember that with all conjugated verbs, the object pronouns go before the verb.

Note also that when **da'**, **di'**, **fa'**, **sta'** are followed by object pronouns, these pronouns take a double consonant: **dammi** (give me), **dillo** (say it), **falle** (do them), etc.

Exercise 7

Answer the questions with the formal form of the imperative and the appropriate object pronoun "lo," "la," "li," "le," "gli." Example:
Che ne pensa, compro la casa?→ Sì, la compri!
What do you think, shall I buy the house? Yes, buy it!

1 Che ne pensa, compro il rustico?
2 Che ne pensa, mangio la minestra?
3 Che ne pensa, parlo alla signora?
4 Che ne pensa, vendo gli appartamenti?
5 Che ne pensa, prenoto le camere?
6 Che ne pensa, faccio la fotografia?
7 Che ne pensa, do la mancia?
8 Che ne pensa, porto i bambini?
9 Che ne pensa, telefono al signor Bianchi?
10 Che ne pensa, prendo l'arrosto?

5

Exercise 8

Reply as in Exercise 7, but this time imagine that the conversation takes place between two friends. Use the familiar form of the imperative and practice answering in both the affirmative and negative. (To find out about the pronoun ne, see page 109.)

Example:
Che ne pensi, compro la casa?→ Sì, comprala!
                                No, non comprarla!

5.4 IRREGULAR VERBS: **BERE, DIRE, SAPERE**

Notice how irregular these three key verbs are in the present tense:

bere (to drink)   **dire** (to say)   **sapere** (to know)

bevo I drink	**dico** I say	**so** I know
bevi	dici	sai
beve	dice	sa
beviamo	diciamo	sappiamo
bevete	dite	sapete
bevono	dicono	sanno

5.5 IRREGULAR PAST PARTICIPLES: **BERE, CUOCERE, DIRE**

	past participle	
bere	**bevuto**	drunk
cuocere	**cotto**	cooked
dire	**detto**	said, told

5.6 TWO WORDS FOR "CAN": **SAPERE, POTERE**

The verb **sapere** is used to indicate that a certain skill or knowledge has been acquired:

So nuotare.
I can swim. (I know how to swim.)
So parlare italiano.
I can speak Italian. (I have learned how to speak it.)
Non so leggere.
I can't read. (I never learned to read.)
But
Non posso nuotare se il mare è mosso.
I can't swim if the sea is rough.
Non posso leggere se non ho gli occhiali.
I can't read if I don't have my glasses.

Exercise 9

Fill in the spaces with the correct form of "sapere" or "potere" in the present tense.

Example:
Non abbiamo la macchina e non … venire.
Non abbiamo la macchina e non possiamo venire.

1 È troppo stanco, non … giocare a tennis.
2 Studio l'italiano e lo … capire abbastanza bene.
3 Prendi lezioni di piano e non … suonare?
4 Vorrei andare al nuovo ristorante ma
   non … dov'è.
5 Il bar è chiuso, [noi] non … prendere la bibita.
6 Mio marito … cucinare bene.
7 Pierino è piccolo e non … ancora scrivere.
8 Scusi, [io] … usare il telefono?
9 Oggi i ragazzi non … nuotare.
10 È pericoloso andare in macchina con Mario:
   non … guidare.

5.7 LIKES AND DISLIKES: **MI PIACE / NON MI PIACE**

To say that you like something in Italian, you use the verb **piacere**. This verb has a different construction from the English "to like," as it literally means "to be pleasing." It is always used with an indirect object pronoun: **mi piace** "it is pleasing to me" or "I like."

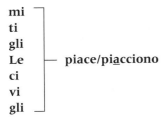

mi
ti
gli
Le   — **piace/piacciono**
ci
vi
gli

The third-person singular **piace** is used when it refers to an action (in the infinitive) or a singular noun:

Le piace l'italiano?
Do you (form.) like Italian? ("Does Italian appeal to you?")
Le piace nuotare?
Do you (form.) like swimming?

and the third-person plural **piacciono** is used when it refers to a plural noun:

Mi piacciono gli spaghetti al dente!
I like spaghetti al dente!

Exercise 10

Answer the following questions using "mi piace" or "mi piacciono." Example:

Le piace quella casa?→ Sì, mi piace moltissimo.
Le piacciono quegli appartamenti?→ Sì, mi piacciono moltissimo.

1 Le piace quel ristorante?
2 Le piacciono le lasagne al forno?
3 Le piace viaggiare?
4 Le piace il vitello?
5 Le piacciono gli zucchini?

and now answer saying what you don't like.

Example:
Le piace questa casa?→ No, non mi piace.
Le piacciono quei rustici?→ No, non mi piacciono.

6 Le piacciono i rumori?
7 Le piace fare niente?
8 Le piacciono le zanzare?
9 Le piace aspettare?
10 Le piacciono le persone noiose?

Da Mamma Rosa

Luigi has invited three of his English friends out for a meal at Mamma Rosa's, a small trattoria in the Trastevere district of Rome, to celebrate his birthday. The owner greets them and takes their order.

ROSA **Buongiorno, signore. Ha prenotato?**

LUIGI **Sì, ho prenotato per quattro.**

ROSA **Prego, accomodatevi qui. Le dico cosa abbiamo oggi, così potete decidere. Volete cominciare tutti con l'antipasto o no?**

LUIGI **Sì, un bell'antipasto misto per tre, ma il mio amico è vegetariano, cosa ci sarebbe per lui?**

ROSA **Abbiamo insalata russa e mozzarella con pomodoro. Va bene?**

LUIGI **Benissimo. E per primo?**

ROSA **Ci sono ravioli di ricotta e spinaci, spaghetti all'Amatriciana e gnocchi alla Romana.**

LUIGI **Gnocchi per due, un piatto di spaghetti per me e i ravioli per la signora, per favore.**

ROSA **E per secondo? Abbiamo trota alla griglia, braciole di maiale e cotolette alla milanese.**

LUIGI **Prendiamo tutti e tre le cotolette, ma è possibile avere un piatto di verdura per il mio amico?**

ROSA **Certo, posso portargli i finocchi al forno, e una bella scelta di altre verdure fresche. E voi cosa prendete di contorno?**

LUIGI **Per noi insalata mista e patate fritte.**

ROSA **E da bere?**

LUIGI **Acqua minerale frizzante e una caraffa di vino rosso della casa.**

At Mamma Rosa's

ROSA   Hello, sir. Have you booked?

LUIGI   Yes, I booked for four.

ROSA   Please take a seat here. I'll tell you what we have today, and then you can decide. Do you all want to start with an antipasto?

LUIGI   Yes, we do, a nice mixed antipasto for three, but my friend is vegetarian, what is there for him?

ROSA   We have Russian salad and mozzarella with tomatoes. Is that all right?

LUIGI   Great. And for the first course?

ROSA   There is ("are") ravioli with ricotta and spinach, spaghetti with Amatriciana sauce, and gnocchi.

LUIGI   Gnocchi for two, spaghetti for me, and ravioli for the lady.

ROSA   And for the main course? We have grilled trout, pork chops, and veal cutlets.

LUIGI   We'll have cutlets for three, but is it possible to have a vegetable dish for my friend?

ROSA   Certainly, I can bring him baked fennel and a nice selection of other fresh vegetables. And what will you have on the side?

LUIGI   Mixed salad and fries for us.

ROSA   And to drink?

LUIGI   Sparkling mineral water and a carafe of red house wine.

Exercise 11

Try to answer these questions about Conversation 3 using object pronouns where possible:

1 Chi vorrebbe solo un piatto di verdura per secondo? E perché?
2 Che cosa c'è di contorno da Mamma Rosa oggi?
3 Prendono tutti i ravioli per primo?
4 Luigi ordina il vino bianco?
5 C'è solo carne per secondo?
6 Quante persone mangiano l'insalata?

5.8 USES OF THE PREPOSITION DA

To talk about going to or staying at someone's house, office, etc., in Italian, you use **da** followed by the person's name or occupation:

Oggi vado dal dentista.
Today I am going to the dentist.
Ieri sono stata da Maria.
Yesterday I stayed at Maria's.
Compro la verdura dal fruttivendolo.
I buy vegetables at the produce market [greengrocer].

Da is also used to describe a continuous period of time (like "for" in English).

Examples:
Da quanto tempo abita a Londra?
How long have you lived in London?
Abito a Londra da tre anni.
I have lived in London for three years.
Studio l'italiano da due mesi.
I have been studying Italian for two months.

Note that with these expressions of time, the present tense must be used in Italian, whereas in English the present perfect tense is required.

Exercise 12

Translate the following sentences:

1 We don't like to travel by train.
2 Do you (fam.) like fries?
3 Please give (form.) this key to signora Rossi.
4 Would you (fam.) go by yourself?
5 Maria, don't take (fam.) my car; take yours.
6 We have given him all the necessary information.
7 Can I offer you (pl.) something to drink?
8 How long have you (pl.) been studying Italian?
9 They would buy the apartment, but it costs €400,000.
10 We went to Tony's for lunch.

Le posso offrire qualcosa?
Mi porti un antipasto misto.
Mario, portagli gli spaghetti!
Non so nuotare.
Mi piacerebbe avere una casa in Italia.

accomodatevi	make yourselves comfortable, sit down
acqua minerale (f.)	mineral water
aglio (m.)	garlic
agnello (m.)	lamb
al dente	slightly undercooked (pasta or rice)
al forno	baked
analcolico	nonalcoholic
antipasto (m.)	starter, hors d'œuvre
antipasto misto (m.)	a variety of cured meats (salami, ham, etc.), olives, etc.
aperitivo (m.)	aperitif
arrosto (m.)	roast
bere	to drink
bianco	white
bibita (f.)	soft drink
bicchiere (m.)	glass
bistecca (f.)	steak
braciola (f.)	chop
caffè (m.)	coffee
caffè corretto (m.)	coffee with a dash of spirits
caraffa (f.)	carafe
carne (f.)	meat
cena (f.)	dinner, supper
cenare	to dine
chiuso	closed
contorno (m.)	side dish
cotoletta (f.)	veal cutlet
cotoletta alla milanese	veal cutlet coated in bread crumbs
cuocere	to cook
cotto	cooked
cravatta (f.)	tie
cucinare	to cook

5

da solo	alone
dentista (m.& f.)	dentist
dire	to say
espresso (m.)	espresso
figurati (fam.)	you're welcome, no problem,
(si figuri form.)	not at all, not to worry
finocchio (m.)	fennel
forno (m.)	oven
fresco	fresh
frizzante	fizzy, sparkling
fruttivendolo (m.)	produce market, greengrocer
giocare	to play (a game)
gnocchi (m. pl.)	potato dumplings
gnocchi alla	semolina dumplings, baked in
romana (m. pl.)	the oven
griglia (f.)	grill
insalata (f.)	salad
insistere	to insist
lasagne (f. pl.)	lasagne
lasciare	to leave, to let
maiale (m.)	pig, pork
mancia (f.)	tip (gratuity)
manzo (m.)	beef
mare (m.)	sea
minerale	mineral
minestra (f.)	soup
mi piace/piacciono	I like (something sing./pl.)
moneta (f.)	loose change, coins
mosso	rough (sea)
noioso	boring
nuotare	to swim
occhiali (m. pl.)	eyeglasses, spectacles
oliva (f.)	olive
osteria (f.)	tavern, pub, bar
patata (f.)	potato
patate fritte (f. pl.)	fries
permettere	to allow
pesce (m.)	fish
piano, pianoforte (m.)	piano
pisello (m.)	pea
pomodoro (m.)	tomato

portare	to bring, to carry
pranzo (m.)	lunch
primo (piatto) (m.)	first course
ravioli (m. pl.)	ravioli
ricotta (f.)	ricotta cheese
rispondere	to reply
rosso	red
russo/a	Russian
Salute!	Cheers!
sapere	to know (how)
scelta (f.)	choice, selection
se	if
secco	dry
secondo (piatto) (m.)	main (second) course
soprattutto	mainly, especially
spaghetti (m. pl.)	spaghetti
specialità (f.)	specialty
suonare	to play (an instrument)
tartina (f.)	canapé, hors d'œuvre
telefonare	to call
tempo (m.)	time (general)
tocca a me	it's my turn
trota (f.)	trout
vegetariano/a	vegetarian
verdura (f.)	vegetable(s)
viaggiare	to travel
vitello (m.)	veal
zanzara (f.)	mosquito
zucchino (m.)	zucchini

5

Week 6

You will learn to:
- buy food, clothes, and presents
- deal with issues at the bank
- ask for your clothing or shoe size
- complain about and return purchases

The grammar will include:
- the direct object pronoun **ne**
- agreement of perfect tenses with pronouns
- double pronouns ("he gives it to me")
- ordinal numbers ("first," "second," "third," etc.)
- irregular verbs: **aprire, chiudere, chiedere, mettere, scrivere, perdere, offrire**

CONVERSATION 1

Dal droghiere / At the grocer

Luisa is doing her daily shopping at the local grocer, Dino's.

DINO   **Buongiorno signorina, desidera?**

LUISA   **Vorrei due etti di prosciutto crudo e un bel pezzo di parmigiano.**

DINO   **Il prosciutto è un po' di più, lascio così? E di parmigiano quanto ne vuole?**

LUISA   **Me ne dia tre, quattro etti. Ma parmigiano reggiano, mi raccomando!**

DINO   **Certo, lo assaggi un po'. Buono eh! E desidera altro?**

LUISA   **Ha la mozzarella?**

DINO   **Sì, ce l'ho di bufala e di mucca.**

LUISA   **Bene, ne prendo due di bufala.**

DINO   **Eccole. Basta così?**

LUISA   **Sì, per oggi sì, quant'è?**

DINO   Good morning, may I help you?

LUISA   I'd like 200 grams of Parma ham and a large piece of Parmesan. [Dino weighs the ham]

DINO   The ham's a bit over. Shall I leave it? And how much Parmesan would you like?

LUISA   Give me 300 or 400 grams. But I want the best Parmesan [from Reggio], mind!

DINO   Certainly, try it. Isn't it good? Anything else?

LUISA   Do you have any mozzarella?

DINO   Yes, I have buffalo's milk and cow's milk mozzarella.

LUISA   Good, I'll take two buffalo ones.

DINO   Here they are. Is that all?

LUISA   Yes, for today. How much is it?

Exercise 1

Read and listen to Conversation 1, then answer the following questions:

1   Dove fa la spesa Luisa?

2   Quanto prosciutto compra?

3   Che parmigiano preferisce?

4   Quante mozzarelle compra?

6.1 THE PRONOUN NE

The pronoun **ne** means:

1 "of it" or "of them":

Quanto pane vuole? Ne voglio un chilo.
How much bread do you want? I want one kilo [of it].
Quanti amici inglesi ha? Ne ho molti.
How many English friends do you have? I have many [of them].

Quante pastine desidera? Ne vorrei tre.
How many pastries do you want? I'd like three [of them].

Note that **ne** must not be omitted in Italian, while "of it" and "of them" are usually omitted in English.

2 "some" or "any" when they are not followed by a noun:

Ha dei francobolli? Sì, ne ho.
Do you have any stamps? Yes, I have some.
Ha del vino? No, non ne ho.
Do you have any wine? No, I don't have any.

3 "about it", "about them":

Chi parla di politica? Tutti ne parlano.
Who's talking about politics? Everyone's talking about it.

Exercise 2

6

Answer these questions using "ne" and the expression given.
Examples:
Quanti francobolli vuole?   ... 4→ Ne vorrei quattro.
Quanti fratelli ha?   ... 1→ Ne ho uno.

1 Quanto olio vuole?   ... un litro.
2 Quanto pane vuole?   ... un chilo e mezzo.
3 Quante mozzarelle vuole? ... una sola.
4 Quanto salame vuole?   ... 2 etti.
5 Quante arance vuole?   ... 2 chili.
6 Quante macchine ha?   ... 1
7 Quanti figli ha?   ... 4
8 Quante scarpe ha?   Non ... molte.
9 Quanti soldi ha?   ... pochi.
10 Quanto tempo ha?   Non ...

6.2 OBJECT PRONOUNS WITH PERFECT TENSES

When direct object pronouns (me, her, etc.) are used with the perfect tenses, the ending of the past participle must change in the same way as when it is used with **essere**:

l'ho visto	I have seen him
l'ho vista	I have seen her
li ho visti	I have seen them (men or men and women)
le ho viste	I have seen them (women)
mi hai visto	you saw me (a man is talking)
mi hai vista	you saw me (a woman is talking)
vi ho visti	I saw you (several men and women or all men)
vi ho viste	I saw you (women)

Note that **li** and **le**, being plural, do not take the apostrophe. Note also that when the object pronoun is indirect—"to me," "to her"—the past participle does not change to agree with it.

Exercise 3

Answer the questions using "lo," "la," "li," or "le" and changing the ending of the past participle if necessary.

Examples:

Hai invitato Maria?→ Sì, l'ho invitata.
Avete comprato le pesche?→ Sì, le abbiamo comprate.

1 Hai invitato tutti gli amici?
2 Hai visitato la galleria?
3 Hai visitato il museo?
4 Hai portato i panini?
5 Hai mangiato le paste?
6 Avete invitato vostra suocera?
7 Avete guardato il catalogo?
8 Avete comprato le riviste?
9 Avete preso la mancia?
10 Avete visto Giovanni?

All'Oviesse

Luisa is buying some presents for her American friends at the Oviesse department store and asks the shop assistant, Carlo, for help with sizes.

LUISA **Vorrei un maglione di lana blù come questo, ma non sono sicura della misura.**

CARLO **È per Lei, signorina?**

LUISA **No, per un'amica americana. Porta il dodici negli Stati Uniti.**

CARLO **Attenda un attimo che controllo. Dunque, il dodici corrisponde al quarantasei in Italia.**

LUISA **Grazie, allora glielo prendo e, scusi, dove sono le pantofole?**

CARLO **Da uomo o da donna?**

LUISA **Da uomo.**

CARLO **Il reparto calzature da uomo è al terzo piano. Sono anche queste per gli amici americani?**

LUISA **Sì, infatti le vorrei chiedere se sa anche le misure delle scarpe.**

CARLO **Sì, ce le ho qui. Il quarantadue italiano è l'equivalente dell'otto americano.**

LUISA **Il mio amico porta l'otto americano.**

CARLO **Allora chieda il quarantadue.**

LUISA **Mille grazie.**

At the Oviesse department store

LUISA I'd like a blue woollen sweater like this one.
But I'm not sure about the size.

CARLO Is it for you?

LUISA No, for an American friend. She takes a 12 in
the United States.

CARLO Wait a minute while I check. So size 12 is the
equivalent of a size 46 in Italy.

LUISA Thank you, then I'll get it for her. And where
are the slippers, please?

CARLO Men's or women's?

LUISA Men's.

CARLO The men's shoe department is on the 3rd floor.
Are these for your American friends, too?

LUISA Yes, in fact, I'd like to ask you if you know about
shoe sizes as well.

CARLO Yes, I have them here. An Italian 42 is the same
as an American 8.

LUISA My friend takes an American 8.

CARLO Then ask for a 42.

LUISA Many thanks.

6

Exercise 4

Read and listen to Conversation 2, then answer these
questions using complete sentences:

1 Che misura vuole Luisa per il maglione?
2 Di che colore lo preferisce?
3 A che piano sono le calzature da uomo?
4 Che misura di scarpe porta l'amico americano?
5 Per chi compra i regali Luisa?

6.3 DOUBLE PRONOUNS ("HE GIVES IT TO ME")

Very often in Italian, two pronouns are used together
before a verb when in English one would be enough:

Glielo prendo.	I'll take it (m.) (for him/her).
Me le mostra?	Will you show (them to) me?
Ce l'ho.	I have it.

When two object pronouns are used together, the direct
object pronoun (**lo**, **la**, **li**, **le**, and **ne**) always follows the
indirect object. In addition, the indirect object pronoun
changes form by replacing -**i** with -**e** (e.g., **mi** > **me**):

```
me  ┐
te  │
glie-├ lo, la, li, le, ne
ce  │
ve  │
glie-┘
```

Note also that **glielo**, **gliela**, **glieli**, **gliele**, **gliene** are
always written as one word, but all the other pronouns
are written as two separate words:

me la da	he gives it (a feminine object) to me
te li da	he gives them (masculine objects) to you (fam.)
ce lo da	he gives it (a masculine object) to us
ve le da	he gives them (feminine objects) to you (pl.)
glielo da	he gives it (masculine object) to you/to her/to him/to them

If these pronouns are followed by a perfect tense, the
past participle needs to agree (see section 6.2):

Glieli ho dati.	I have given them (**i giornali**) to him.
Te le ho scritte.	I have written them (**le lettere**) to you.

Exercise 5

Answer these questions addressed to you, using "glielo," "gliela," "glieli," "gliele," or "gliene":

Examples:
Porta la rivista a Maria?→ Sì, gliela porto.
Porta il giornale a Maria?→ Sì, glielo porto.

1 Porta i panini ai ragazzi?
2 Scrive la lettera a Maria?
3 Dà il conto alla signora?
4 Dà i soldi alla signora?
5 Porta il vestito al signor Bianchi?
6 Scrive le lettere a tutti?
7 Compra la pasta per gli ospiti?
8 Compra i grissini per Maria?
9 Vende l'appartamento a questi signori?
10 Vende la casa a questi signori?

Exercise 6

Now put the questions (this time posed by a friend) and answers in Exercise 5 in the present perfect tense to talk about the past:

Examples:
Hai portato la rivista a Maria?→ Sì, gliel'ho portata.
Hai portato il giornale a Maria?→ Sì, gliel'ho portato.

Exercise 7

Answer these questions using the appropriate double pronouns.

Examples:
Chi ti ha fatto la spesa? ... il ragazzo. → Me l'ha fatta il ragazzo.

Chi vi ha offerto un aperitivo? ... Maria.→ Ce l'ha offerto Maria.

1 Chi ti ha consigliato questo ristorante? ... un'amica.
2 Chi ti ha dato l'indirizzo? ... il poliziotto.
3 Chi ti ha portato la valigia? ... il facchino.
4 Chi ti ha riparato l'orologio? ... l'orologiaio.
5 Chi ti ha mandato i fiori? ... un amico.
6 Chi vi ha portato l'antipasto? ... il cameriere.
7 Chi vi ha venduto le matite? ... la commessa.
8 Chi vi ha comprato quei regali? ... nostra figlia.
9 Chi vi ha prenotato l'albergo? ... l'agenzia.
10 Chi vi ha dato la moneta? ... l'impiegata.

Exercise 8

Answer these questions addressed to you, using the formal "Lei" form of the imperative and the appropriate double pronouns.

Example:
Glielo mando io?→ Sì, me lo mandi pure.
(Do I send it to you?)→ (Yes, send it to me.)

1 Glielo porto io?
2 Glieli mando io?
3 Gliele regalo io?
4 Gliela scrivo io?
5 Glielo prenoto io?

Exercise 9

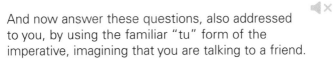

And now answer these questions, also addressed to you, by using the familiar "tu" form of the imperative, imagining that you are talking to a friend.

Example:
Te lo porto io? → Sì, portamelo pure!

1 Te la preparo io?
2 Te le mando io?
3 Te li compro io?
4 Te lo scrivo io?
5 Te la prendo io?

CONVERSATION 3

Alla banca

Tony has used his credit card at the ATM outside the Banca del Lavoro in Verona, but has not managed to get any money out, so he goes inside the bank to ask the cashier what to do:

TONY **Scusi, ho provato a usare la mia carta di credito al Bancomat qui fuori, ma non sono riuscito a ritirare i soldi.**

CASSIERE **Ha mai usato la Sua carta di credito in Italia?**

TONY **Sì, a Rimini e non ho mai avuto difficoltà.**

CASSIERE **Mi dica cos'ha fatto.**

TONY **Ho messo la carta dentro, poi ho digitato il mio codice segreto, ho premuto il tasto verde e ...**

CASSIERE **E non ha funzionato?**

TONY **Gliel'ho già detto. Sullo schermo c'è scritto che ho aspettato troppo e poi si è chiusa la grata e basta!**

CASSIERE **Di solito quando c'è scritto così è perché ha dimenticato di premere qualche tasto.**

TONY   Ho capito. Allora, che cosa mi consiglia di fare?

CASSIERE   Provi un'altra volta, ma stia attento e prema il tasto verde subito.

TONY   Va bene, ma se la macchina non mi dà i soldi, me li può dare Lei?

CASSIERE   Certo, non si preoccupi!

TRANSLATION 3

At the bank

TONY   Excuse me, I tried to use my credit card at the ATM outside, but I couldn't get any money out (lit. "didn't manage to withdraw the money").

TELLER   Have you ever used your ATM card in Italy?

TONY   Yes, in Rimini, and I have never had any problems.

TELLER   Tell me what you did.

TONY   I put my card in, then punched in my PIN number, pressed the green button, and ...

TELLER   Did it not work, then?

TONY   I've already told you that. On the screen, it said that I had waited too long, then the shutter came down and that was it!

TELLER   Usually when it says that, it's because you forgot to press some button.

TONY   I see. So what do you advise me to do?

TELLER   Try once more, but be careful and press the green button immediately.

TONY   OK, but if the machine doesn't give me the money, can you give it to me?

TELLER   Of course, don't worry!

Exercise 10

Read and listen to Conversation 3, then answer the following questions:

1 Dove ha messo la carta di credito Tony?

2 Che cosa c'è scritto sullo schermo?

3 La grata del Bancomat è chiusa adesso?

4 Tony ha perso i soldi?

5 Perché Tony è entrato in banca?

6.4 ORDINAL NUMBERS (FIRST, SECOND, ETC.)

Ordinal numbers are used in Italian in the same way as in English, with the exception of days of the month (see section 4.8). Here are the first 10:

1st	**primo**	6th	**sesto**
2nd	**secondo**	7th	**settimo**
3rd	**terzo**	8th	**ottavo**
4th	**quarto**	9th	**nono**
5th	**quinto**	10th	**decimo**

All other ordinal numbers are formed by removing the ending of the cardinal number and adding **-esimo**:

11th	**undicesimo**
12th	**dodicesimo**
25th	**venticinquesimo**
1,000th	**millesimo**

Note that ordinal numbers have feminine and plural endings, like all other adjectives ending in **-o**. Examples:

Te lo dico per la centesima volta.
I am telling you for the hundredth time.
Papa Giovanni Ventitreesimo
Pope John XXIII
il tredicesimo secolo
the 13th century

Exercise 11

Translate the following sentences:

1 The shoe department is on the 10th floor.
2 This is the sixth week.
3 The 1st of May is a national holiday in Italy.
4 We live in the 21st century.
5 Take (formal) the fourth street on your left.

6.5 IRREGULAR VERBS: **APRIRE, CHIEDERE, CHIUDERE, METTERE**, ETC.

The present perfect of these verbs is formed in the usual way, by using the present tense of **avere** plus the past participle. But notice the latter's irregularity in each case:

	present perfect
aprire (to open)	**ho aperto** (I opened)
chiedere (to ask)	**ho chiesto** (I asked)
chiudere (to close)	**ho chiuso** (I closed)
mettere (to put)	**ho messo** (I put)
scrivere (to write)	**ho scritto** (I wrote)
perdere (to lose)	**ho perso** (I lost)
offrire (to offer)	**ho offerto** (I offered)

CONVERSATION 4

Da Garda Moda / At the Garda Moda boutique

Jeff bought a shirt in a small boutique in Garda, but when he got back home, he found that they had given him the wrong size. He asks the shop assistant (**commessa**) to change it.

JEFF **Ho comprato questa camicia stamattina e vorrei cambiarla perché è la taglia sbagliata.**

COMMESSA **Ma non l'ha provata prima?**

JEFF **No, ma ho chiesto il quarantadue e questo è il quaranta.**

COMMESSA **Mi dispiace, signore, ma non abbiamo un quarantadue in quel colore.**

JEFF **Allora mi può dare indietro i soldi?**

COMMESSA **Vede, c'è scritto qui: 'Non si fanno rimborsi'. Ma Le posso dare un altro colore.**

JEFF **No, è colpa vostra che mi avete dato la taglia sbagliata. Se non avete la mia taglia, voglio indietro i soldi.**

COMMESSA **Guardi, telefono all'altro nostro negozio e se neanche loro ce l'hanno, Le do un buono che può usare per qualsiasi artícolo.**

JEFF **No, voglio i soldi o la camicia. Per favore, chiami il proprietario.**

TRANSLATION 4

JEFF I bought this shirt this morning, and I would like to change it because it's the wrong size.

SHOP ASSISTANT Didn't you try it on first?

JEFF I didn't, but I asked for a size 42 and this is a 40.

SHOP ASSISTANT I'm sorry, sir, but we don't have a 42 in that color.

JEFF Then can you give me my money back?

SHOP ASSISTANT	Look, it says here: "We don't give refunds." But I can give you another color.
JEFF	No, it's your fault, you gave me the wrong size. If you don't have my size, I want my money back.
SHOP ASSISTANT	Look, I'll call our other shop and if they don't have it either, I'll give you a voucher, which you can use to buy any other article.
JEFF	No, I want either the money or the shirt. Please call the owner.

Exercise 12

Put the following passage into the present perfect, changing "oggi" into "ieri" and changing the endings of the past participles where necessary. Begin like this:

Ieri Tony e Luisa sono andati alla Rinascente ...

Oggi Tony e Luisa vanno alla Rinascente per comprare due regali: uno per la madre di Tony e l'altro per quella di Luisa. Luisa va al pianterreno, al reparto accessori, e compra una borsetta di pelle. Tony va a dare un'occhiata al reparto casalinghi al sesto piano. Guarda i servizi da tè e da caffè, ma non li compra.

Alle quattro Tony e Luisa vanno a prendere il tè in un bar in Piazza del Duomo e Luisa gli fa vedere la borsetta. Dopo due ore decidono di tornare alla Rinascente perché Luisa vede che la cerniera della borsetta è rotta. La porta indietro all'Ufficio Reclami e chiede un rimborso dei soldi o un'altra borsetta. L'impiegato le domanda la ricevuta e dopo molte difficoltà le dà una borsetta nuova. Tony nel frattempo guarda dappertutto, ma non trova niente per la madre di Luisa.

Questo non è un pomeriggio molto fortunato per i due giovani!

Me ne dia due etti.
Perché non gliele hai date?
Ho chiesto indietro i soldi.
Questa è la sesta settimana.

accessori (m. pl.)	accessories
aprire	to open
arancia (f.)	orange
articolo (m.)	article, item
assaggiare	to taste
attendere	to wait
attimo (m.)	minute, moment
Bancomat	ATM
basta	it's enough
blu	blue
borsetta (f.)	handbag
bufalo/a	buffalo
buono (m.)	voucher
calzature (f. pl.)	footwear
cambiare	to change
camicia (f.)	shirt
capitolo (m.)	chapter
carta di credito (f.)	credit card
cassiere/a	cashier, teller
catalogo (m.)	catalog
cerniera (f.)	zip, zipper
chiedere	to ask
chilo (m.)	kilo(gram)
chiudere	to close
codice segreto (m.)	PIN number
colore (m.)	color
colpa (f.)	fault
come	like
comprare	to buy
conto (m.)	bill
corrispondere	to be the equivalent of
dentro	inside
difficoltà (f.)	difficulty
digitare	to key in

6

droghiere (m.)	grocer
etto (m.)	100 grams
facchino (m.)	porter
festa (f.)	feast, party
fortunato	lucky
francobollo (m.)	postage stamp
funzionare	to work, function
giovane	young
grammo (m.)	gram
grata (f.)	shutter
grissino (m.)	breadstick
impiegato/a (m./f.)	clerk, employee
indietro	back
in tutto	altogether
lana (f.)	wool
lettera (f.)	letter
magazzino (m.)	store
maglione (m.)	sweater
mandare	to send
matita (f.)	pencil
mettere	to put
Mi raccomando!	Mind!, Be sure to ..., Don't forget!
misura (f.)	size
moneta (f.)	loose change
mucca (f.)	cow
nazionale	national
nel frattempo	in the meantime
occhiata (f.)	look, glance
olio (m.)	oil
orologiaio/a	watchmaker
pane (m.)	bread
panino (m.)	bread roll, sandwich
pantofole (f. pl.)	slippers
Papa (m.)	pope
parmigiano (m.)	Parmesan
pastina (f.)	pastry
pelle (f.)	leather
perdere	to lose
pezzo (m.)	piece
piacevole	pleasant
politica (f.)	politics

6

pomeriggio (m.)	afternoon
portare	to bring, to carry, to wear
portare indietro	to bring back
premere	to press
proprietario/a	owner
prosciutto (m.)	ham
reclami (m. pl.)	complaints
regalare	to give (as a present)
regalo (m.)	present
reparto (m.)	department
ricevuta (f.)	receipt
rimborso (m.)	refund
riparare	to mend
ritirare	to withdraw
riuscire	to succeed, to manage to
rivista (f.)	magazine
rotto	broken
salame (m.)	salami
sbagliato	wrong
scarpe (f. pl.)	shoes
schermo (m.)	screen
secolo (m.)	century
segreto	secret
servizio (m.)	set, service
soldi (m. pl.)	money
spendere	to spend
spesa (f.)	shopping (for food)
spese (f. pl.)	purchases, shopping
stamattina	this morning
suocero/a	father/mother-in-law
taglia (f.)	size
tasto (m.)	button, key
usare	to use
vestito (m.)	dress, suit
visitare	to visit

6

Week 7

You will learn to:

▨ say how you feel and describe ailments
▨ report an accident
▨ name parts of the body

The grammar will include:

▨ reflexive verbs ("I enjoy myself")
▨ imperfect and past perfect tenses ("I was doing," "I had done")
▨ irregular plurals
▨ irregular verbs: **correre, rimanere, rispondere, rompere, sedersi, succedere**

CONVERSATION 1

In ambulatorio

Tony Jones has gone to see Dr. Guglielmini with a severe stomachache.

DOTTORE	**Si accomodi, signor Jones. Come si sente?**
TONY	**Ho mal di stomaco da due giorni e mi fa veramente male.**
DOTTORE	**Dov'è il dolore di preciso?**
TONY	**Qui, proprio in alto, e non mi passa neanche se mi corico.**
DOTTORE	**Si metta sul lettino che La visito.** **[Dopo la visita]**
DOTTORE	**Bene, si vesta e si sieda qui che Le spiego.**
TONY	**Allora, cosa ne pensa?**
DOTTORE	**Secondo me, Lei ha una forma leggera di gastroenterite.**
TONY	**Ma è una malattia seria!**
DOTTORE	**Non si preoccupi, prenda questa medicina tre volte al giorno dopo i pasti per una settimana e poi torni da me.**
TONY	**Grazie.**
DOTTORE	**Prego, e non si preoccupi!**

At the doctor's office

DOCTOR Sit down, Mr. Jones. How do you feel?

TONY I've had a stomachache for two days, and it's really hurting me.

DOCTOR Where exactly is the pain?

TONY Here, up high, and it doesn't go away even when I lie down.

DOCTOR Lie on the examination table and I'll take a look. [After the examination]

DOCTOR Right, get dressed and come and sit down while I explain.

TONY So what do you think (about it)?

DOCTOR In my opinion, you have a mild form of gastroenteritis.

TONY But that's a serious illness!

DOCTOR Don't worry: take this medicine three times a day after meals for a week, and then come back to see me.

TONY Thank you.

DOCTOR You're welcome, and don't be concerned!

7

Exercise 1

Read and listen to Conversation 1, then answer the following questions:

1 Perché Tony va dal dottore?

2 Secondo Lei, Tony si preoccupa molto?

3 Quante volte al giorno deve prendere la medicina?

4 Quando deve tornare dal dottore?

5 Tony ha una malattia seria?

7.1 REFLEXIVE VERBS ("I ENJOY MYSELF")

In Italian, verbs used with a reflexive pronoun to indicate
that the subject is performing the action on itself (such as
"I enjoy myself," "I dress myself," etc.) are much more
common than in English. These infinitives always end in
the pronoun **si**. They include:

1 Verbs that are reflexive in both languages:

divertirsi	to enjoy oneself
farsi male	to hurt oneself
lavarsi	to wash oneself
vestirsi	to dress oneself

2 Verbs that are reflexive in Italian, but not in English:

addormentarsi	to fall asleep
alzarsi	to get up
ammalarsi	to fall ill
chiamarsi	to be called
coricarsi	to lie down
dimenticarsi	to forget
ricordarsi	to remember
riposarsi	to rest
sedersi	to sit down
svegliarsi	to wake up

... including many verbs that in English start with
"to get ...":

annoiarsi	to get bored
arrabbiarsi	to get angry
perdersi	to get lost
preoccuparsi	to get/be worried
sposarsi	to get married
stancarsi	to get tired
svestirsi	to get undressed

All reflexive verbs must be preceded by the relevant reflexive pronoun—this can't be omitted:

present tense

mi lavo	I wash myself
ti lavi	you wash yourself
si lava	he washes himself/she washes herself/you (form.) wash yourself
ci laviamo	we wash ourselves
vi lavate	you wash yourselves
si lavano	they wash themselves

All reflexive verbs form the perfect tenses with **essere**, and the ending of the past participle must agree with the reflexive pronoun:

present perfect

mi sono lavato/a	I washed myself
ti sei lavato/a	you washed yourself
si è lavato/a	he washed himself/she washed herself/you (form.) washed yourself
ci siamo lavati/e	we washed ourselves
vi siete lavati/e	you washed yourselves
si sono lavati/e	they washed themselves

Remember that the reflexive pronouns must <u>always</u> be expressed in Italian, even when the verb is followed by a direct object:

Ci siamo lavati.
We washed ourselves.
Mi sono lavato le mani.
I washed my hands.
Si è fatta male al ginocchio.
She hurt her knee.

Note also that the definite article, not the possessive adjective, is then used to refer to the part of the body, since it is clear whose it is.

7

Exercise 2

Answer these questions addressed to you in the formal, using the reflexive verb and the given phrase.

Example:

Quando si rade? ... ogni mattina.→ Mi rado ogni mattina.

When do you shave? ... every morning.→ I shave every morning.

1	Quando si alza ?	... alle 8.
2	Quando si corica?	... alle 11.
3	Quando si lava?	... tutte le mattine.
4	Quando si stanca?	... a lavorare troppo.
5	Quando si arrabbia?	Non ... mai.
6	Quando si annoia?	... a far la coda.
7	Quando si diverte?	... in vacanza.
8	Quando si sveglia?	... alle 7.30.
9	Quando si riposa?	... dopo pranzo.
10	Quando si perde?	... se non ho la cartina.

7

Exercise 3

Complete the following sentences using these verbs:

addormentarsi	to fall asleep
farsi male	to get hurt
sentirsi bene	to feel well
sentirsi male	to feel unwell
ricordarsi	to remember
dimenticarsi	to forget
sposarsi	to get married
ammalarsi	to fall ill
lavarsi	to wash
asciugarsi	to dry oneself

Make sure that you use the same person and tense as in the first part of the sentence.

Examples:

Se siamo stanchi ...→ Se siamo stanchi ci riposiamo.

Quando ho lavorato per 10 ore ...→ Quando ho lavorato per 10 ore mi sono stancato/a.

1 Quando cado ...

2 Quando sono andati a letto ...

3 Ieri è andata dal dottore perché ...

4 Maria è stata a letto quando ...

5 Abbiamo fatto il bagno, poi ...

6 Non ti ho telefonato perché ...

7 Maria e Giovanni sono andati in chiesa e ...

8 Non prendo più le medicine perché ...

9 Quando sono sporchi ...

10 Se scrivo la lista della spesa ...

7

Un incidente stradale

Peter describes to his girlfriend, Luisa, a road accident he saw in the center of Rome:

PETER Scusami per il ritardo, ma c'è stato un brutto incidente davanti all'università.

LUISA Un incidente? Cos'è successo?

PETER Mentre aspettavo l'autobus ho visto un mio compagno che è stato investito da un motorino.

LUISA Il tuo compagno attraversava la strada?

PETER Sì, ha visto l'autobus arrivare e si è messo a correre, ma c'era un motorino che veniva da una strada laterale e lui non se n'è accorto.

LUISA Mamma mia, si è fatto male?

PETER Ho proprio paura di sì, io sono corso subito per aiutarlo. Forse si è rotto una gamba.

LUISA Avete chiamato l'ambulanza?

PETER Sì, ed è venuta subito. L'hanno portato al Pronto Soccorso dell'ospedale.

LUISA Se vuoi, possiamo andare a trovarlo oggi pomeriggio.

7

TRANSLATION 2

A road accident

PETER   I'm sorry I'm late, but there was a bad accident in front of the university.

LUISA   An accident? What happened?

PETER   While I was waiting for the bus, I saw one of my friends get hit by a scooter.

LUISA   Was your friend crossing the road?

PETER   Yes, he saw the bus coming, and he started to run, but there was a scooter coming from a side street and he didn't notice it.

LUISA   Oh dear! Was he hurt?

PETER   I'm really afraid he was. I immediately ran over to help him. He may have broken his leg.

LUISA   Did you call an ambulance?

PETER   Yes, and it came right away. They've taken him to the ER at the hospital.

LUISA   If you want, we could go and visit him this afternoon.

Exercise 4

Read and listen to Conversation 2, then answer the following questions:

1 Perché Peter è in ritardo?

2 Che cosa è successo al suo compagno?

3 Perché il suo compagno non ha visto il motorino?

4 Dove l'hanno portato?

5 Dov'era Peter quando è successo tutto questo?

The imperfect tense is formed by removing the final **-re** of the infinitive and adding the endings **-vo**, **-vi**, **-va**, **-vamo**, **-vate**, **-vano**:

parlare	vedere	venire
parlavo	vedevo	venivo
parlavi	vedevi	venivi
parlava	vedeva	veniva
parlavamo	vedevamo	venivamo
parlavate	vedevate	venivate
parlavano	vedevano	venivano

The imperfect tense is used to describe a regular or repeated action in the past. For example:

1 to describe people or things:

Garibaldi aveva la barba.
Garibaldi had a beard.

2 to describe habitual or continuous action, as in the English "I used to do" or "I was doing":

Maria mangiava quando sono arrivato.
Maria was eating when I arrived.
Da piccola abitavo in campagna.
As a child, I used to live in the country.

3 to describe something that happened in the past and went on for an unspecified period of time:

I bambini non volevano uscire.
The children did not want to go out.

7.3 USE OF PERFECT AND IMPERFECT TENSES

To help know which of these two past tenses to use, remember: the perfect is used for a one-off action in the past, while the imperfect is used when the action went on for an unspecified period of time:

Ho mandato una lettera a Maria perché non stava bene. I sent a letter to Maria because she wasn't well.

ho mandato:	a completed one-off action
stava:	a description of a state over an unspecified period of time

7.4 IMPERFECT OF **ESSERE**

This very common verb is irregular in the imperfect.

ero	I was
eri	you were
era	he/she/it was
eravamo	we were
eravate	you were
erano	they were

7

Exercise 5

Answer these questions addressed to you in the informal and plural, using the imperfect tense:

Andavi a scuola quando eri piccolo/a?→ Sì, andavo a scuola quando ero piccola/o.

Andavate a scuola quando eravate piccoli?→ Sì, andavamo a scuola quando eravamo piccoli.

1 Studiavi quando eri piccolo?
2 Facevi molti sport quando eri a scuola?
3 Viaggiavi molto quando abitavi in Italia?
4 Andavi sempre in macchina quando lavoravi in centro?
5 Sentivi molto i rumori quando dormivi al pianterreno?
6 Facevate molte gite quando eravate in montagna?
7 Andavate fuori spesso quando abitavate a Milano?
8 Guidavate quando avevate 18 anni?
9 Mangiavate solo verdura quando vivevate in Inghilterra?
10 Compravate sempre il giornale quando lavoravate in Italia?

7

Exercise 6

Answer the following questions using "ero" or "eravamo" and the given phrases. Examples:

Perché non sei venuto ieri? ... impegnato.→ Perché ero impegnato.
(Why didn't you come yesterday?)→ (Because I was busy.)
Perché non siete venuti ieri? ... impegnati.→ Perché eravamo impegnati.

1 Perché sei andato all'ospedale? ... malato.
2 Perché non hai scritto? ... indisposto.
3 Perché non hai telefonato? ... arrabbiato.
4 Perché non sei venuto prima? ... troppo stanco.
5 Perché non hai visto il motorino? ... distratto.
6 Perché non avete preso il caffè? ... senza soldi.
7 Perché siete andati dal dottore? ... malati.
8 Perché non siete venuti? ... stanchi.
9 Perché non vi siete fermati di più? ... in ritardo.
10 Perché avete chiamato l'ambulanza? ... molto preoccupati.

Exercise 7

Transform these sentences using the imperfect to say what used to be the case. Example:

Adesso non leggo più.→ Una volta leggevo molto.
Now I don't read any more.→ Once I used to read a lot.

1 Adesso non viaggiate più.
2 Adesso non ci preoccupiamo più.
3 Adesso non viaggiano più.
4 Adesso non scrivi più.
5 Adesso non lavora più.
6 Adesso non mi diverto più.
7 Adesso non usciamo più.
8 Adesso non fumo più.
9 Adesso non leggi più.
10 Adesso non parlano più.

Exercise 8

Put these sentences into the past tense using "ieri," making sure that you use both the perfect and imperfect tenses where necessary. Example:

Prende un'aspirina perché non si sente bene.→ Ieri ha preso un'aspirina perché non si sentiva bene.

1 Prendo l'autobus perché sono stanca.
2 Non guardo la televisione perché non funziona.
3 Sono a Firenze e vado agli Uffizi.
4 Noi andiamo dal dottore perché abbiamo la febbre.
5 Il dottore ti visita a casa quando sei a letto malata.
6 Mi alzo alle dieci perché è festa.
7 Mentre leggo il giornale entra il mio ospite.
8 Mentre scrivo la lettera i bambini mangiano tutti i cioccolatini.
9 Sandra ha mal di testa e non va a lavorare.
10 Mentre cammino lungo la strada vedo un incidente.

7.5 IRREGULAR PLURALS

PARTS OF THE BODY

When describing parts of the body, take care because many have irregular plurals and some also change from masculine to feminine in the plural:

l'orecchio (m.)	le orecchie (f.)	ears
il labbro (m.)	le labbra (f.)	lips
il braccio (m.)	le braccia (f.)	arms
il dito (m.)	le dita (f.)	fingers
il ginocchio (m.)	le ginocchia (f.)	knees
la mano (f.)	le mani (f.)	hands

Examples:
Giovanni si è fatto male alle ginocchia.
Giovanni hurt his knees.
Ho le dita gelate.
My fingers are frozen.

Note that unlike in English, the definite article rather than a possessive adjective is used with parts of the body (see the note at the end of section 7.1).

MORE IRREGULAR PLURALS

Some other irregular plurals include the following:

1 Masculine words ending in **-a** change to the ending **-i** in the plural:

il programma	i programmi
il telegramma	i telegrammi
l'artista	gli artisti
il pianista	i pianisti
il violinista	i violinisti

2 Foreign words, words ending with an accented vowel, words ending in **-i**, and abbreviated words remain unchanged in the plural:

la città	le città
la difficoltà	le difficoltà
l'hobby	gli hobby
il taxi	i taxi
la tesi (thesis)	le tesi
il bar	i bar
il caffè	i caffè
la radio	le radio

7

CONVERSATION 3

In farmacia

Jeff is asking the pharmacist (**farmacista**) for advice after getting badly burnt by the sun.

FARMACISTA **Desidera?**

JEFF **Vorrei una crema contro le scottature.**

FARMACISTA **Si è proprio preso una bella scottatura al viso.**

JEFF **Non solo al viso, ma anche sulla schiena e sulle gambe.**

FARMACISTA **Le do questo pomata. Se la metta due volte al giorno, ma stia attento a non esporsi al sole.**

JEFF **Va bene, grazie. E quanto devo evitare il sole?**

FARMACISTA **Finché l'arrossamento non è passato. Se poi si spella torni da me che Le do un'altra pomata protettiva.**

JEFF **Grazie mille.**

TRANSLATION 3

At the pharmacist's

PHARMACIST May I help you?

JEFF I'd like a cream to relieve ("against") sunburn.

PHARMACIST You've certainly burned your face badly.

JEFF Not only my face, but my back and legs, too.

PHARMACIST I'll give you this cream. Apply it twice a day, but be careful and don't expose yourself to the sun.

JEFF All right, thank you. How long should I avoid the sun?

PHARMACIST Until all the redness has gone. Then if it peels, come back and I'll give you another protective salve.

JEFF Thank you.

Exercise 9

Read and listen to Conversation 3, then answer
these questions:

1 Perché Jeff va dalla farmacista?
2 Che cosa gli prescrive?
3 Dove si deve mettere la pomata?
4 Fino a quando deve evitare il sole?
5 Poi che cosa deve fare?

Exercise 10

Complete the following conversation using the
clues given:

YOU   Buongiorno, dottore.
DOCTOR Buongiorno, si accomodi. Che disturbi ha?
YOU   (I have a backache.)
DOCTOR Da quanto tempo ha questi sintomi?
YOU   (For two days.)
DOCTOR Vediamo. Si corichi sul lettino e mi dica
        se Le fa male.
YOU   (Yes, it is very painful. Is it serious?)
DOCTOR No, non si preoccupi! Dovrebbe essere solo
        uno strappo muscolare.
YOU   (What is a "muscle strain"? What shall I do?)
DOCTOR Uno strappo muscolare è abbastanza comune.
        Si riposi il più possibile e se deve piegarsi,
        pieghi le ginocchia e non la schiena.
YOU   (Could you give me something for the pain?)
DOCTOR Le do questa medicina per rilassare i muscoli.
YOU   (Thank you, doctor!)

7

7.6 MORE IRREGULAR VERBS

Note the irregular present tense of the reflexive verb **sedersi** (to sit down). Below that are some verbs with irregular past participles—some form the perfect tenses with **avere**, others with **essere** (see section 3.6 if you need a reminder about this).

present tense of **sedersi**
mi siedo
ti siedi
si siede
ci sediamo
vi sedete
si siedono

		present perfect
correre	to run	**ho corso / sono corso/a**
rimanere	to stay	**sono rimasto/a**
rispondere	to reply	**ho risposto**
rompere	to break	**ho rotto**
succedere	to happen	**è successo** (it happened)

7.7 PAST PERFECT ("I HAD DONE")

This tense ("I had seen," "I had gone") is used in Italian in the same way as it is in English—to express an action that happened before another action in the past. It is formed by using the imperfect tense of the verbs **avere** or **essere** and the past participle:

Avevo già chiamato l'ambulanza quando sei arrivato tu.
I had already called an ambulance when you arrived.
Non era ancora andata a trovarlo.
She had not gone to see him yet.

Exercise 11

Put the verbs in brackets into the past perfect in the following sentences.

Example:

Ieri Anna (andare) dal signor Bianchi, così io sono rimasta sola.→ Ieri Anna era andata dal signor Bianchi, così io sono rimasta sola.

1 Eva non (rispondere) alla mia lettera, così non le ho più scritto.

2 Gli studenti (andare) a Firenze due altre volte, ma questa volta hanno visto gli Uffizi.

3 Voi (essere) in casa tutto il tempo e non me l'avete detto?

4 Il dottore (scrivere) la ricetta lunedì, ma l'ho ricevuta oggi.

5 Maria non (rompere) mai niente, ma oggi ha fatto un disastro!

6 Silvio (farsi male) al braccio, così non è potuto venire.

7 Che cosa (succedere), perché non sei andato?

8 La macchina si è fermata perché io non ci (mettere) benzina.

9 Ha detto che (chiudere) la porta.

10 Noi (sedersi) già, quando sei entrato tu.

KEY PHRASES & VOCABULARY

Non è venuto perché era stanco.
Si sono fatti male alle braccia.
Tony ha detto che il motorino l'aveva investito.
Tutti i taxi erano occupati.

addormentarsi	to fall asleep
ambulanza (f.)	ambulance
ambulatorio (m.)	doctor's office, clinic
aiutare	to help
accorgersene	to notice
alzarsi	to get up
ammalarsi	to fall ill
annoiarsi	to get bored
artista (m. & f.)	artist
asciugarsi	to get dry
arrabbiarsi	to get angry
arrabbiato	angry
arrossamento (m.)	reddening
attraversare	to cross
aver male di	to have a pain in …
barba (f.)	beard
benzina (f.)	gasoline
braccio (m.) (pl. -a f.)	arm
brutto	ugly
camminare	to walk
campagna (f.)	countryside
chiamarsi	to call oneself, to be called
cioccolatini (m. pl.)	chocolates
compagno/a	friend, mate
coricarsi	to lie down
correre	to run
crema (f.)	cream
di preciso	exactly
distratto	absent-minded, distracted
dito (m.) (pl. -a f.)	finger, toe
divertirsi	to enjoy oneself
dolore (m.)	pain
dottore / dottoressa	doctor
esporsi al sole	to sunbathe, to be exposed to sun

7

evitare	to avoid
finché … non	until
farmacista (m. & f.)	pharmacist
far male	to hurt
febbre (f.)	fever, temperature
festa (f.)	feast (day), holiday, party
forma (f.)	form
forse	perhaps
gamba (f.)	leg
gastroenterite (f.)	gastroenteritis
gelato	frozen
ginocchio (m.) (pl. **-a** f.)	knee
guidare (m.)	to drive
hobby (m.)	hobby
impegnato	busy, engaged
incidente (m.)	accident
indisposto	indisposed, unwell
investire	to run over, to hit
labbro (m.) (pl. **-a** f.)	lip
laterale	on the side
lavarsi	to wash oneself
leggero	light, mild
letto (m.)	bed
lettino (m.)	examination table, couch
malattia (f.)	illness, disease
male (m.) (**di** …)	ache, pain
mano (m.) (pl. **-i** f.)	hand
medicina (f.)	medicine
medico/a	medical doctor
medico	medical
motorino (m.)	scooter
orecchio (m.) (pl. **-e** f.)	ear
ospedale (m.)	hospital
passare	to pass, to go
perdersi	to get lost
pianista (m. & f.)	pianist
pomata (f.)	ointment
preoccuparsi	to be worried
preoccupato	worried
prescrivere	to prescribe
programma (m.)	program

7

Pronto Soccorso (m.)	ER, critical care
protettivo	protective
radersi	to shave
ricetta (f.)	prescription
rimanere	to stay
riposarsi	to rest
rompere	to break
schiena (f.)	back
scottatura (f.)	burn
secondo	according to, in the opinion of
sedersi	to sit down
sentirsi	to feel
serio	serious
sole (m.)	sun
spellarsi	to peel
spiegare	to explain
sporcarsi	to get dirty
sporco	dirty
sposarsi	to get married
stancarsi	to get tired
stomaco (m.)	stomach
strada (f.)	road
strappo muscolare (m.)	muscular sprain
subito	immediately
succedere	to happen
svegliarsi	to wake up
svestirsi	to undress
telegramma (m.)	telegram
testa (f.)	head
una volta	once
uscire	to go out
vestirsi	to get dressed
violinista (m. & f.)	violinist
visita (f.)	visit, examination
visitare	to visit, to examine
viso (m.)	face

7

Week 8

You will learn to:
- talk about hobbies and interests
- express opinions about shows, films, performances, etc.
- arrange meetings and activities
- agree or disagree and apologize
- write a letter

The grammar will include:
- comparatives and superlatives ("more," "most," "less", "least", "as")
- prepositions followed by infinitives
- expressions using **avere**
- agreement and disagreement
- use of the verb **fare**
- irregular verb: **accorgersi**

CONVERSATION 1

Alla festa

Fabio and Marina are at a party, where they have just been introduced. They discuss their mutual interests.

FABIO **Le piace il calcio?**

MARINA **No, non mi interesso di sport, e Lei?**

FABIO **Beh, sono un tifoso dell'Inter, ma la mia vera passione è la lirica.**

MARINA **Ma davvero? Anche a me piace molto. Specialmente Puccini.**

FABIO **Qual è il Suo cantante preferito?**

MARINA **Per me Placido Domingo è insuperabile. Ma anche Andrea Bocelli è bravo, intendiamoci.**

FABIO **Bravo? È unico! È il miglior tenore del mondo.**

MARINA **In un certo senso, sì. Tecnicamente è bravissimo. Ma Domingo ha una voce più calda, più espressiva.**

FABIO **In questo Le do ragione. Domingo è molto espressivo e recita anche bene. Ma ha visto Bocelli alla televisione ieri?**

8

MARINA   **Sì, per dire la verità, mi è piaciuto.**
FABIO   **Vede? Gliel'ho detto che è un genio!**

TRANSLATION 1

At the party

FABIO   Do you like soccer?
MARINA   No, I'm not interested in sports, and you?
FABIO   Well, I'm a fan of Inter Milan, but opera is my real passion.
MARINA   Really? I like it a lot, too. Especially Puccini.
FABIO   Who is your favorite singer?
MARINA   For me, Placido Domingo is unbeatable. But Andrea Bocelli is good, too, let's face it (lit. "we understand each other").
FABIO   Good? He is unique! He's the best tenor in the world.
MARINA   In a way, yes. Technically, he is very good. But Domingo's voice has more warmth, more feeling.
FABIO   You're right about that. Domingo sings with feeling and acts well, too. But did you see Bocelli on TV yesterday?
MARINA   Yes, I must admit, I liked him.
FABIO   See? Didn't I tell you that he is a genius!

Exercise 1

1 Secondo Marina, Bocelli è bravo come Domingo?
2 Perché Fabio non è d'accordo?
3 Tecnicamente, chi canta meglio?
4 A Marina è piaciuto Bocelli alla televisione?
5 Marina è appassionata di sport?
6 Per chi fa il tifo Fabio?

COMPARATIVES OF INEQUALITY: "MORE/ LESS ... THAN"

In Italian, when comparing two things that are unequal, the word **più** (more) or **meno** (less) is placed in front of the adjective or adverb:

Ha una voce più espressiva.
He has a more expressive voice.
È una strada meno affollata.
It is a less crowded street.
Guardo la televisione più spesso.
I watch television more often.

"Than" is translated by:

1 di before a noun, pronoun, or number:

Il film dura meno di un'ora.
The film lasts less than one hour.
Tutti si divertono più di me.
They are all enjoying themselves more than me.
Capisco Maria più facilmente di Gino.
I understand Maria more easily than Gino.

2 che before any other part of speech:

Questa storia è più tragica che comica.
This story is more tragic than comic.
Vado a teatro più spesso d'inverno che d'estate.
I go to the theater more often in winter than in summer.

Note that if two similar things with different qualities are being compared, **che** is used even before nouns:

Ci sono più turisti che veronesi in città.
There are more tourists than Veronese in town.
Leggo più riviste che giornali.
I read more magazines than newspapers.

8

COMPARATIVES OF EQUALITY: "AS … AS"

When comparing two things that are alike ("as … as"), in Italian you don't translate the first "as" and you use **come** to translate the second:

Milano è grande come Roma.
Milan is as big as Rome.
Milano non è grande come Londra.
Milan is not as big as London.

Note that when in English you use "as much" or "as many," in Italian you use **tanto … quanto**, but these agree with the noun or pronoun they refer to:

Ho tanto tempo quanto te.
I have as much time as you.

Ho tanti amici quanti te.
or, more commonly,
Ho tanti amici quanto te.
I have as many friends as you.

8

Exercise 2

Fill in the gaps in the following sentences using "più di" or "più che." Example:
Luisa guadagna ... ... 2000 euro al mese.→ Luisa guadagna più di duemila euro al mese.

1 Ci sono ... ... 30.000 spettatori all'Arena.
2 Secondo me Roma è ... grande ... Milano.
3 Giovanni è ... studioso ... intelligente.
4 Ci sono ... teatri a Roma ... a Torino.
5 Conosco ... attori italiani ... stranieri.
6 Sua figlia è ... alta ...lei.
7 Fa ... caldo in Italia ... in Inghilterra.
8 Parla ... piano ... me.
9 Luisa mangia ... ... tutti.
10 L'Aida mi piace ... ... Rigoletto.

8.2 SUPERLATIVES (MOST, LEAST)

The superlative is formed in Italian by putting **il più, la più, i più, le più** ("the most" or "-est" in English) in front of the adjective:

Il Panteon aveva la più grande cupola del mondo.
The Pantheon had the largest dome in the world.

The English "in" is translated by **di** after a superlative.

SUPERLATIVES ENDING IN -ISSIMO

To say that something is very big, very easy, etc. in Italian, you can either use **molto** or add **-issimo/a/i/e** to the end of the adjective:

This opera is very long.	**Quest'opera è molto lunga.**
or	**Quest'opera è lunghissima.**
The palaces are very old.	**I palazzi sono molto vecchi.**
or	**I palazzi sono vecchissimi.**

8

8.3 IRREGULAR COMPARATIVES AND SUPERLATIVES

buono	**migliore**	**ottimo**
good	better/best	very good
cattivo	**peggiore**	**pessimo**
bad	worse/worst	very bad
grande	**maggiore**	**massimo**
great	greater/greatest	very great
piccolo	**minore**	**minimo**
small	smaller/smallest	very small

molto	much	**più**	more/most
poco	a little	**meno**	less/least
bene	well	**meglio**	better*
male	badly	**peggio**	worse*

* These are used only as adverbs.

Examples:
Zia Teresa è il miglior ristorante di Napoli.
Zia Teresa is the best restaurant in Naples.
Il Barolo è un ottimo vino.
Barolo is a very good wine.
I miei fratelli minori sono a scuola.
My younger brothers are at school.
Canta meglio di me.
He sings better than me.

Note that **minore** "smaller" and **maggiore** "greater" can also mean "younger" and "older," respectively.

The word **migliore** "better/best" can drop the final **e** when followed by another word. The same is true of many other Italian words that end in **-re**:

È il peggior film del festival.
It is the worst film in the festival.
Penso di andar via.
I am thinking of leaving.
Parlo al signor Rossi.
I am speaking to Mr. Rossi.

Exercise 3

Translate the following sentences:

1 This is the worst wine in the world!
2 We are as good as you (pl.) in Italian.
3 There were more than 20,000 spectators.
4 Maria Callas was a very famous singer.
5 St. Paul's (Cathedral) is not as big as St. Peter's.
6 Giovanni drinks more coffee than water.
7 I feel better now.
8 These programs are very boring.
9 We did not buy as many presents as you (pl.).
10 My younger sister lives in Milan.

CONVERSATION 2

In Piazza San Marco

Tony and Luisa have come to Venice for the day. Luisa wants to visit a church with her friend Carla, and Tony wants to go to an exhibition.

TONY **Allora, se vuoi andare alla Chiesa del Carmine con Carla io mi fermo a vedere la mostra.**

LUISA **Poi dove ci troviamo?**

TONY **Fra due ore davanti all'Accademia?**

LUISA **Va bene.**
      [Due ore dopo]

LUISA **Eccoci qua, ti è piaciuta la mostra?**

TONY **Sì, moltissimo. E voi, vi siete divertite?**

LUISA **Sì. L'Assunzione del Tiziano era magnifica. Poi, per strada, abbiamo fatto anche delle compere.**

TONY **Davvero? Cosa avete comprato?**

LUISA **Dei regali per i nostri amici.**

TONY **Bene. Ma non avete fame adesso?**

8

LUISA **Sì, molto. Abbiamo visto una trattoria qui vicino, perché non ci andiamo insieme?**

TONY **Volentieri. Ho proprio voglia di sedermi e riposarmi un po'.**

LUISA **Ottima idea. Andiamo!**

TRANSLATION 2

In St. Mark's Square

TONY So if you want to go to the Chiesa del Carmine with Carla, I'll stay and see the exhibition.

LUISA Where shall we meet* afterward?

TONY In two hours in front of the Accademia?

LUISA OK.

[Two hours later]

LUISA Here we are—did you like the exhibition?

TONY Yes, very much. And you, did you enjoy yourselves?

LUISA Yes, Titian's Assumption was superb. Then on the way back, we also did some shopping.

TONY Did you? What did you buy?

LUISA Some presents for our friends.

TONY Good. Aren't you hungry now?

LUISA Yes, very. We saw a trattoria near here; why don't we go there together?

TONY I'd love to. I really feel like sitting down and resting for a while.

LUISA Excellent idea! Let's go!

* The verb "to meet" can be translated by **trovarsi** to describe an arranged meeting, or by **incontrarsi** to describe a chance meeting, i.e., to run into ("encounter") someone.

Exercise 4

Read and listen to Conversation 2, then answer the following questions:

1 Che cosa vuole vedere Tony?
2 Perché non ci va anche Luisa?
3 Dove si trovano fra due ore?
4 Che cosa hanno comprato le due ragazze?
5 Dove vanno a mangiare?

8.4 PREPOSITIONS WITH INFINITIVES

In Italian, "to" before an infinitive is:

1 Not translated with modal verbs such as **voglio, posso, devo** as well as **preferisco, mi piace, desidero**:

Preferisco stare a casa.
I prefer to stay at home.
Non mi piace camminare.
I don't like to walk.

2 Translated by **a** with verbs such as **andare, venire, restare, imparare, divertirsi, riuscire**:

Vado a vedere la mostra.
I'm going to see the exhibition.
Comincio a capire.
I'm beginning to understand.
Li invito a mangiare.
I'm inviting them to eat.

3 Translated by **di** with verbs such as **finire, pensare, credere, accorgersi, promettere, decidere, sperare**:

Ha deciso di venire.
He decided to come.

Finisco di leggere.
I'll just finish (lit. "I finish") reading.
Penso di venire.
I'm thinking of coming.

Note that in English, verbs preceded by prepositions end in-ing, but in Italian the infinitive is used:

Ha cominciato a criticare.
He started criticizing.

Unfortunately, there is no rule to help you know which verbs are preceded by **a** and which by **di**. You'll get the hang of this through practice: try to take note of the preposition when a verb is used.

Exercise 5

Complete the following sentences with the verbs provided, using the correct prepositions (if required) before the infinitive:

1 Maria e Gianni (decided to) non uscire oggi.

2 (We start) camminare alle tre.

3 (She hopes) arrivare in tempo.

4 (I don't like) guardare la partita di calcio.

5 (Do you enjoy) (familiar) visitare i musei e le gallerie?

6 (He prefers) fare le compere.

7 Tutti i negozi (must) chiudere una volta alla settimana.

8 (I finished) scrivere la lettera.

9 (They think) capire molto ma non capiscono niente.

10 (We are going) mangiare al ristorante.

8.5 APOLOGIZING

To say that you're sorry, you use **dispiacere**, which is constructed with an indirect object pronoun: **mi dispiace**, i.e., "it is displeasing to me":

mi dispiace	I am sorry
ti dispiace	you are sorry
gli dispiace	he is sorry
le dispiace	she is sorry
Le dispiace	you are sorry (form.)
ci dispiace	we are sorry
gli dispiace	they are sorry

Mi dispiace, ma non posso fermarmi.
I'm sorry, but I can't stay.
Ci dispiace di essere in ritardo.
We're sorry we're late.

LETTER-WRITING PRACTICE

Tony is writing to his teacher to apologize for not attending his classes.

Venezia, 24 settembre 2021

Caro Professore,

Sono venuto a Venezia con la mia ragazza e avevamo pensato di tornare domenica sera. Purtroppo, però, non possiamo arrivare in tempo per la lezione d'italiano lunedì perché la nostra amica ci ha gentilmente invitati a restare qui ancora per qualche giorno per vedere la Regata storica.

Abbiamo deciso di accettare perché non vogliamo perdere l'occasione di vedere uno spettacolo unico al mondo come questo. La prego di accettare le mie scuse per questa assenza.

8

Mi dispiace molto di dover perdere le lezioni e vorrei pregarLa di tenermi i fogli delle lezioni di lunedì, se questo non Le è di troppo disturbo.

Distinti saluti

Tony Smith

TRANSLATION

Venice, 24 September 2021

Dear Professor,

I came to Venice with my girlfriend, and we had thought of coming back on Sunday evening. Unfortunately, however, we can't be back in time for the Italian lesson on Monday because our friend has kindly invited us to stay here for a few more days to see the historic Regatta.

We have decided to accept as we don't want to miss the opportunity to see such a unique spectacle [in the world]. Please accept my apology for this absence.

I am very sorry to have to miss classes, and I'd like to ask you to keep Monday's worksheets for me if it's not too much trouble for you.

Yours sincerely,

Tony Smith

NOTE: a formal letter usually starts with **Caro** (or **Egregio**), **Cara** (or **Gentile**) followed by the addressee's title (**Dottore, Signore, Dottoressa**, etc.) and ends with **Distinti saluti** (Yours faithfully/sincerely). A less formal letter starts with **Caro/Cara** followed by the addressee's first name and ends with **Tanti saluti** or **Affettuosi saluti** (Love, Much love). The address is usually put at the bottom of a letter.

8

Exercise 6

Translate the following letter of apology:

Dear Mr. Rossi,

Thank you for your invitation to the theater next Tuesday. I'm sorry, but unfortunately I can't come. I am going to Florence on Tuesday, and I'm unable to come back until Wednesday.

Please accept my apologies, but I have to go on business and I can't refuse.

Yours sincerely,

8.6 EXPRESSIONS USING AVERE

There are many expressions in Italian using **avere** that in English would use the verb "to be":

avere ragione	to be right
avere torto	to be wrong
avere fame	to be hungry
avere sete	to be thirsty
avere freddo	to be cold
avere caldo	to be hot
avere paura	to be afraid
avere fretta	to be in a hurry
avere voglia	to be willing/to feel like

Examples:
Mario ha ragione e tu hai torto.
Mario is right and you are wrong.
Io ho fame e freddo.
I am cold and hungry.

8

There are a couple of ways to say you agree with someone: **essere d'accordo** or **dare ragione.** To disagree, use **non essere d'accordo** or **dare torto**.

Examples:
Maria ha ragione, ma Antonio le dà sempre torto.
Maria is right, but Antonio always disagrees with her.
Sono d'accordo con te.
I agree with you.

Note: **essere d'accordo con ...** *but* **dare ragione a ...**

Exercise 7

Comment on the statements using the correct expression from the following:

avere fame	avere caldo
avere sete	dare ragione
avere ragione	dare torto
avere torto	avere fretta
avere freddo	avere paura

Example:
Dico che la regina d'Inghilterra si chiama Rita. Io ho torto.

1 Oggi la temperatura è sotto zero. Io ...
2 Non mangiano da due giorni. (loro) ...
3 Mario dice che io sono molto bravo. Io ... !
4 Tutti dicono che Maria studia poco, ma Maria ...
5 A Napoli ci sono 40 gradi. Tutti ...
6 Vogliamo una bottiglia di acqua minerale. (noi) ...
7 Mario pensa sempre di aver ragione, ma io ...
8 Non mi piace viaggiare da sola perché (io) ...
9 Devono correre a prendere il treno. (loro) ...
10 Silvia dice che Parigi è in Spagna. Silvia ...

8

8.8 USE OF THE VERB **FARE**

The verb **fare** is also used in many expressions, with different meanings:

1 "to do" and "to make":

Faccio il tè.   I'm making tea.
Che cosa fai?   What do you do?
Faccio fatica.   I'm making an effort.

2 "to be" with jobs and professions:

Faccio la commessa.
I am a shop assistant.

3 "to take":

Faccio una passeggiata.
I'm taking a walk.
Faccio il bagno.
I'm taking a bath.

4 "to give":

Ho fatto una conferenza su Dante.
I gave a lecture on Dante.

5 "to get something done":

Faccio riparare la televisione.
I'm getting the TV repaired.
Li faccio studiare.
I make them study.
Mi fa fare tutto!
He makes me do everything!

8

6 to describe the weather:

Fa bel tempo.	The weather is nice.
Fa freddo.	It is cold.

7 in idiomatic expressions:

fare attenzione	to pay attention
far figura/colpo	to impress
fare la coda	to queue
fare il tifo	to support, to cheer
farcela	to manage
farla a qualcuno	to trick/deceive somebody
far sapere	to inform, to let [someone] know

8.9 IRREGULAR VERB: ACCORGERSI

The verb **accorgersi** (to notice) has an irregular past
participle, which you need to know for the perfect tenses.

	present perfect	
accorgersi	**mi sono accorto/a**	I noticed

Exercise 8

Answer the following questions using the correct form of "fare" and a pronoun to replace the noun.

Examples:

Allora ce l'avete fatta?→ Sì, ce l'abbiamo fatta.
  (Could you manage then?)→ (Yes, we managed.)

Fa l'attrice Lei?→ Sì, faccio l'attrice.
  (Are you an actress?)→ (Yes, I'm an actress.)

1 Avete fatto una passeggiata?
2 Hai fatto molte lezioni?
3 Fa brutto tempo oggi?
4 Ti fa ripetere l'esercizio?
5 Mi fa vedere quella fotografia?
6 Fate colazione in albergo?
7 Ti fai costruire una casa?
8 Vi fa fare molto lavoro?
9 Ce la fai?
10 Avete fatto fatica?

Exercise 9

Translate the following sentences:

1 We decided to go to the exhibition.
2 In my opinion, this is Fellini's worst film.
3 They didn't realize that I was very tired.
4 Which is the largest theatre in the world?
5 I don't like music as much as you (fam.) do.
6 Hotels are more expensive in August than in June.
7 Shall we meet in three hours?
8 I'm very sorry to be late.
9 Did you enjoy yourself (fam.) with your friends yesterday?
10 Did you (formal) manage to find the tickets?

8

Mi dispiace di non essere venuta.
È il più famoso cantante del mondo.
Non ce la faccio più.
Londra è più grande di Milano.

accettare	to accept
accordo (m.)	agreement
accorgersi	to realize, to notice
affettuoso	affectionate, loving
appassionato	fond, keen
assenza (f.)	absence
attore / attrice	actor / actress
aver voglia (di)	to feel like, to want
bravo	good, clever
calcio (m.)	soccer
caldo	hot, warm
cantante (m. & f.)	singer
cattivo	bad
coda (f.)	queue
compera (f.)	purchase
conferenza (f.)	lecture
costruire	to build
criticare	to criticize
cupola (f.)	dome
davvero	really
dispiacersi	to be sorry
distinto	distinguished
Distinti saluti	Yours sincerely/faithfully
disturbo (m.)	bother, disturbance
duomo (m.)	cathedral
Egregio	Dear [sir]
espressivo	intense, with feeling
facilmente	easily
fame (f.)	hunger
fatica (f.)	effort
farcela	to manage, to cope
fermarsi	to stop, to stay
festa (f.)	party
festival (m.)	festival

8

Firenze (f.)	Florence
fissare	to arrange
freddo	cold
fretta (f.)	hurry
galleria (f.)	gallery
genio (m. & f.)	genius
Gentile	Dear [madam]
gentile	kind
grado (m.)	degree
incontrarsi	to meet
insuperabile	unbeatable, outstanding
intelligente	intelligent, clever
intendere	to understand
interessarsi	to be interested
inverno (m.)	winter
invito (m.)	invitation
lirica (f.)	operatic music, opera
maggiore	greater/older, greatest/oldest
magnifico	magnificent
male	badly
meglio	better (adverb)
migliore	better, best
minore	smaller, smallest/younger, youngest
musica (f.)	music
mondo (m.)	world
mostra (f.)	exhibition
museo (m.)	museum
occasione (f.)	opportunity
palazzo (m.)	palace, apartment complex
passatempo (m.)	pastime
passeggiata (f.)	walk
passione (f.)	passion, interest
paura (f.)	fear
peggio	worse (adverb)
peggiore	worse
per affari	on business
pessimo	very bad
pregare	to pray, to beg
presuntuoso	conceited
ragione (f.)	right, reason

8

recitare	to act
regata (f.)	regatta
Roma (f.)	Rome
saluto (m.)	greeting
scusare	to forgive, to excuse
senso (m.)	way, sense
sete (f.)	thirst
simpatico	likable
sincero	sincere
sotto	below, under
Spagna (f.)	Spain
spesso	often
spettacolo (m.)	show, spectacle
spettatore / spettatrice	spectator, viewer
storia (f.)	story, history
storico	historical
straniero/a	foreign, foreigner
studioso	studious
tanto … quanto	as much … as
teatro (m.)	theater
tecnicamente	technically
tenore (m.)	tenor
tifo (m.)	cheer
fare il tifo	to support, to cheer
tifoso/a	fan, supporter
torto	wrong
tragico	tragic
trovarsi	to meet
turista (m. & f.)	tourist
unico	unique
verità (f.)	truth
voce (f.)	voice

8

Week 9

You will learn to:
- describe your job and talk about jobs in general
- choose the appropriate form of address
- discuss current affairs
- spell names, acronyms, and email addresses

The grammar will include:
- relative pronouns ("who," "whom," "which," "that," etc.)
- imperatives of **fare, dire, andare**
- **da', di', fa', sta', va'** with pronouns
- the present participle or gerund (English "-ing" form)
- present and past continuous (**sto/stavo** + present participle), to be about to (**stare per** …)
- negative pronouns and adverbs ("nothing," "no one," "never")
- irregular verbs: **eleggere** and verbs ending in **-gliere**

CONVERSATION 1

A una riunione di ex-allievi

At a school reunion, Antonio and Maria meet up again 10 years after leaving school and talk about their jobs.

ANTONIO **Ciao Maria, ti ho riconosciuta subito!**

MARIA **Ciao, mi pareva di averti riconosciuto. Sono proprio contenta di rivederti.**

ANTONIO **Anch'io, sai. E dimmi un po', cosa fai di bello?**

MARIA **Faccio l'avvocata, e tu? Ti sei dedicato agli affari, mi pare.**

ANTONIO **Sì, lavoro per una compagnia che fabbrica computer.**

MARIA **Li fai o li vendi?**

ANTONIO **Li vendo, lavoro nel reparto vendite. È Marco che è diventato un esperto di elettronica. Ti ricordi di Marco, no?**

MARIA **Come no? È lui che mi ha fatto conoscere mio marito!**

ANTONIO **Davvero? Tuo marito era all'università con lui?**

9

MARIA **No, no. Mio marito gestisce un bar, ma vanno spesso in piscina insieme e ci siamo conosciuti lì.**

ANTONIO **Fammi conoscere tuo marito, e io ti presento la mia compagna. È quella che parla con Tina e Mario.**

MARIA **Benissimo. Chi è la signora con cui parla Sandro?**

ANTONIO **Quella è la direttrice della nostra società. Era un anno avanti a noi a scuola.**

TRANSLATION 1

At a school reunion

ANTONIO Hello, Maria, I recognized you right away!

MARIA Hi! I thought I recognized you. I'm really happy to see you again.

ANTONIO So am I, you know. Tell me, what do you do now?

MARIA I'm a lawyer, and you? You're in business, aren't you?

ANTONIO Yes, I work for a computer manufacturing company.

MARIA Making or selling them?

ANTONIO I sell them. I work in the sales department. It's Marco who's become an expert in electronics. You remember Marco, don't you?

MARIA Of course I do! He's the one who introduced me to my husband.

ANTONIO Really? Was your husband at college with him?

MARIA No. My husband runs a bar, but they often go to the swimming pool together and we met there.

ANTONIO Introduce me to your husband, and I'll introduce you to my partner. She's the one talking to Tina and Mario.

MARIA Great. Who is the lady Sandro is talking to?

ANTONIO She's our company manager. She was in the year above us at school.

Exercise 1

Read and listen to Conversation 1, then answer these questions using complete sentences:

1 Cosa fa il marito di Maria?
2 Qual è la compagna di Antonio?
3 Chi è Marco?
4 Che cosa fa Antonio?
5 È Marco che fa l'avvocato?

9.1 RELATIVE PRONOUNS: WHO, WHICH, THAT, ETC.

While relative pronouns are sometimes omitted in English, in Italian they are always expressed.

Here are the key relative pronouns:

1 che is the equivalent of "who," "whom," "which," "that" when these are not used with a preposition:

la signora che è venuta
the lady who came
gli uomini che hai conosciuto
the men (whom) you met
gli uffici che restano aperti
the offices that stay open

2 cui is used after a preposition or to translate "whose":

Questa è la ditta per cui lavoro.
This is the firm I work for ("for which I work").
i colleghi con cui lavoro
the colleagues with whom I work
È Marco di cui conosco la moglie.
It's Marco whose wife I know.

9

3 quello che or **ciò che** when the relative pronoun "what" in English is used with the meaning of "that which":

Faccio quello che vuoi.
I'll do what you want.
Ciò che vedi è ciò che ho.
What you see is what I have.
Ti do tutto quello che ho.
I'll give you all I have.

4 quelli che (plural) or **chi** (singular) to translate the English "that/those/the one/ones/he/she/they/someone who/whoever …"

Chi non paga non può venire.
Whoever doesn't pay can't come.
Quelli che non pagano non possono venire.
Those who don't pay can't come.

However, this is the only time **chi** is used as a relative pronoun. Otherwise, it is used only in questions (see Week 2): **chi** must NEVER be used instead of **che**.

5 il quale (which also takes the forms **la quale**, **i quali**, **le quali** and combines with the prepositions **a**, **di**, **da**, **in**, **su**) is used almost exclusively in writing. It is usually used for emphasis or to avoid ambiguity:

il padre della signora, del quale ti ho parlato
the lady's husband, about whom I spoke to you
questi colleghi, ai quali non parlo
these colleagues, to whom I don't talk

9

Exercise 2

Complete these sentences using the correct form of the relative pronouns "che," "cui," "quello che," "quelli che," "chi," "il/la quale":

1 Quella signora ... parla con Maria è la mia capa.

2 Questa è la Borsa di Milano di ... ti ho parlato.

3 Molti degli uffici in ... lavoriamo sono al primo piano.

4 Mi dice sempre ... vuole.

5 ... non studiano non passano gli esami.

6 Lo stipendio ... riceviamo è minimo.

7 Per favore mi potete mandare tutto ... avete preparato?

8 La ragazza di Antonio, con ... non parlo più, è simpatica invece.

9 Questo è l'albergo in ... siamo stati durante le vacanze.

10 ... non ha visto Roma non conosce l'Italia.

9

Tony is asking Luisa when she uses **tu** and when she uses **Lei**.

TONY Dimmi Luisa, tu a chi dai del tu e a chi del Lei?

LUISA Dunque, io do del tu a tutti i giovani della mia età e naturalmente ai miei parenti, anche a quelli più anziani.

TONY E io a chi potrei dare del Lei?

LUISA Fa' come me. Da' del tu a tutti eccetto alle persone che non conosci e che sono decisamente più vecchie di te.

TONY Per esempio, il giornalaio ti ha dato del tu, ma tu gli hai dato del Lei. Come mai?

LUISA Il giornalaio mi conosce da quand'ero bambina, ma io, essendo più giovane, devo dargli del Lei.

TONY Ho capito. Allora io posso dare del tu alla cameriera della mensa che ha più o meno la mia età?

LUISA Beh, dipende. Se ti dà del tu, dalle del tu, altrimenti no.

TONY Mi pare una cosa un po' delicata!

LUISA Sì, è una questione un po' personale. Sta' attento, se non sei sicuro usa il Lei.

TONY Tell me, Luisa, who do you use **tu** with and who do you use **Lei** with?

LUISA Well, I use **tu** with all young people of my age, and of course with my relatives, even elderly ones.

TONY What about me? Who should I use **Lei** with?

LUISA Do what I do. Use **tu** with everybody except people whom you don't know and who are definitely older than you.

TONY For instance, the newsdealer used **tu** with you, but you used **Lei** with him. Why?

LUISA The newsdealer has known me since I was a child, but being younger, I have to use **Lei** with him.

TONY I understand. So can I use **tu** with the canteen waitress who is roughly my age?

LUISA Well, it depends. If she uses **tu** with you, you do the same; otherwise, you don't.

TONY It seems a bit tricky to me!

LUISA Yes, it's quite a personal thing. Be careful, and if you're not sure, use **Lei**.

Exercise 3

Read and listen to Conversation 2, then answer these questions using full sentences whenever possible:

1 A chi dà del tu Luisa?
2 Perché le dà del tu il giornalaio?
3 A chi potrebbe dare del tu Tony?
4 A chi dovrebbe dare del Lei?
5 Luisa dà del Lei a Tony?

9

IRREGULAR VERBS: IMPERATIVES OF
ANDARE, DIRE, FARE

	andare	dire	fare
	(to go)	(to say)	(to do)
tu	vai/va'!	di'!	fai/fa'!
Lei	vada!	dica!	faccia!
noi	andiamo!	diciamo!	facciamo!
voi	andate!	dite!	fate!

Examples:
Signora, vada all'ufficio passaporti!
Please go to the passport office, madam!
Fatelo adesso, ragazzi!
Do it now, boys!
Mi dica la verità, signor Rossi!
Tell me the truth, Mr. Rossi!

9.3 **SHORTENED IMPERATIVES WITH PRONOUNS**

When **dai/da'**, **di'**, **fai/fa'**, **stai/sta'**, and **vai/va'**—
shortened imperative forms—are used with an object
pronoun, the initial consonant of the pronoun is doubled
(except for **gli**):

Dacci oggi il nostro pane quotidiano.
Give us today our daily bread.
Dille la verità!
Tell her the truth.
Fammi un favore!
Do me a favor!
Stacci almeno un'ora.
Stay there at least an hour.
Valli a trovare in agosto.
Go and visit them in August.

Note that **ci** means "there" as well as "us" and "to us."
The expression **andare a trovare** means "to pay a
visit to."

9

Exercise 4

Change these imperatives from the "lei" to the "tu" form.

Example:
Mi faccia un favore! → Fammi un favore!

1 Mi dia quell'indirizzo.
2 Le faccia vedere l'ufficio.
3 Ci dica la verità!
4 La vada a trovare domani.
5 Mi dia del tu!
6 Ci stia un po' di più!
7 Le faccia il biglietto.
8 Mi dica chi è!
9 Gli faccia una fotografia.
10 Mi dia la mano!

9

Il programma d'attualità

Peter and his landlady are discussing a current affairs
program they've just watched on television.

PETER   **Se ho capito bene l'euro sta salendo rispetto
al dollaro.**

PADRONA   **Sì, certo che, considerando il costo della
vita, probabilmente tutto rimane lo stesso.**

PETER   **Ma il Presidente del Consiglio ha spiegato
che se gli stipendi non aumentano, anche i
prezzi restano uguali.**

PADRONA   **Mah! I sindacati stanno discutendo proprio
adesso un aumento del sette per cento.**

PETER   **Secondo Lei i sindacati avrebbero torto?**

PADRONA   **No, ma gli stipendi dovrebbero restare al di
sotto dell'inflazione.**

PETER   **L'inflazione è più bassa in Italia che in
America, vero?**

PADRONA   **Sì, al momento sì. Ma ha visto che c'è lo
sciopero dei treni domani?**

PETER   **Di tutti i mezzi di trasporto, mi pare. Di
solito quanto durano questi scioperi?**

PADRONA   **Lo sciopero generale di solito dura solo
ventiquattr'ore.**

PETER   **Meno male! Perché vorrei andare via per il
weekend. Ma, a dir la verità, io sono
d'accordo con i ferrovieri.**

PADRONA   **Ah si? E perché?**

PETER   **Il loro portavoce ha detto che fanno
sciopero perché prendono in media uno
stipendio di soli millecinquecento euro al
mese. Non è molto.**

PADRONA   **Vedo che Lei è di sinistra. Come mio figlio.
Io sono di destra, invece.**

PETER   **In un certo senso sì, in America voto
democratico.**

9

A current affairs program

PETER If I understood correctly, the euro is going up against the dollar.

LANDLADY Yes, it is. But considering the cost of living, it's all likely to stay the same.

PETER But the prime minister explained that if wages don't go up, prices will stay the same, too.

LANDLADY Who knows! The unions are discussing a 7 percent pay rise at the moment.

PETER In your opinion, are the unions wrong?

LANDLADY No, but wages ought to stay below inflation.

PETER Inflation is lower in Italy than in America, isn't it?

LANDLADY Yes, at the moment it is. But did you see that there is a train strike tomorrow?

PETER An all-out transportation strike, I think. How long are these strikes usually?

LANDLADY A general strike usually lasts only 24 hours.

PETER Thank goodness for that! Because I'd like to go away for the weekend. But, quite frankly, I agree with the railroad workers.

LANDLADY You do, do you? Why?

PETER Their spokesperson said that they are striking because they get on average only 1,500 euros a month. That's not much.

LANDLADY I see that you are left-wing. Like my son. I myself am on the right, however.

PETER In a way, yes. In America, I vote Democrat.

9

Exercise 5

Read Conversation 3 and check any new expressions, then try to answer these questions without looking back at the text:

1 L'euro sta scendendo?
2 Peter è di destra?
3 Perché fanno sciopero i ferrovieri?
4 Il costo della vita sta salendo in Italia?
5 Di che cosa stanno parlando Peter e la signora?

9.4 THE PRESENT PARTICIPLE (-ING FORM)

In Italian, the present participle or gerund (the "-ing" form in English: "going," "doing," "surfing," etc.) is formed by removing the **-o** ending from the first-person present tense and adding **-ando** (for **-are** verbs) or **-endo** (for **-ere** and **-ire** verbs):

parlare	vedere	uscire
parlando	**vedendo**	**uscendo**
speaking	seeing	going out

While the endings of the present participle are never irregular, with verbs that are irregular (such as **bere**, **dire**, etc.), remember that the stem is formed from the first-person present and not from the infinitive:

bere	**(io bevo)**	**bevendo**
dire	**(io dico)**	**dicendo**
fare	**(io faccio)**	**facendo**

Examples:
Camminando in fretta sono arrivata in cinque minuti.
(By) walking fast, I arrived in 5 minutes.
Uscendo ho visto Paola.
(When) going out, I saw Paola.

9

As you can see in the previous examples, the -ing form of the verb in Italian is used without an adverb. Also, if a preposition is required before the verb, then you must use an infinitive (see section 8.4).

Note also that in Italian, the infinitive is used rather than a gerund (an -ing verb used as a noun):
Fumare fa male.
Smoking ("To smoke") is harmful.
And an -ing verb is never used in a relative clause:
la ragazza che parla con lui
the girl who is talking ("talks") with him

9.5 PRESENT AND PAST CONTINUOUS

To say that you are or were doing something, the present or past continuous (also known as the present or past progressive) is used.

In Italian, these are formed with the present or imperfect of **stare** (not **essere**), followed by the present participle:

sto mangiando	**stavo mangiando**
I am eating	I was eating
stai	**stavi**
sta	**stava**
stiamo	**stavamo**
state	**stavate**
stanno	**stavano**

However, the continuous tenses are much less commonly used in Italian than in English. As a general rule, they are used only to emphasize what is happening at a precise moment, i.e., to be in the middle of doing something:

Non può venire adesso, sta mangiando.
He can't come now; he's eating.
Stiamo partendo proprio adesso.
We are leaving right now.

9

Stavo uscendo e proprio allora ha suonato il telefono.
I was going out and just then the phone rang.

Note that object pronouns can be put either before **stare** or at the end of the present participle:

La sto guardando.
or **Sto guardandola.**
I am looking at her.

Exercise 6

Complete the following sentences by adding the present participle of the verbs given in brackets:

1 Maria e Giovanni stavano (guardare) la partita alla televisione.
2 (studiare) i verbi ho imparato a parlare meglio.
3 (leggere) il giornale seguo le notizie d'attualità.
4 Ho visto il suo vestito (mettere) via la roba.
5 Aspetta, non vedi che l'ascensore sta (venire).
6 Ha fatto i soldi (vendere) frutta e verdura al mercato.
7 Non posso venire al bar, il treno sta (arrivare) proprio adesso.
8 Abbiamo passato la serata (discutere) di politica.
9 (fare) colazione al bar arrivo in ufficio presto.
10 Che cosa ti stavano (dire)?

9

9.6 USE OF **STARE PER ...**

When you want to say that something is just about to or going to happen, in Italian you use **stare per ...** followed by an infinitive.

Fammi sedere! Sto per svenire.
Let me sit down! I am going to faint.
Il treno sta per fermarsi.
The train is about to stop.

9.7 IRREGULAR VERB: **ELEGGERE**

eleggere (to elect)

present perfect: **ho eletto** I elected

9.8 NEGATIVE PRONOUNS AND ADVERBS: NOTHING, NO ONE, NEVER, ETC.

In Italian, all negative pronouns, such as **niente** (nothing), **nessuno** (no one), **mai** (never), **neanche** (neither, not even), **né ... né** (neither ... nor), etc. require **non** before the verb:

Non conosco nessuno a Roma.
I don't know anyone in Rome.
Non siete mai andati al Vaticano?
Have you never been to the Vatican?
Non mangio né carne né pesce.
I eat neither meat nor fish.
Non ci credo neanch'io.
I don't believe it either.

Note that in Italian, you can use two or more negatives in the same sentence:

Non mangia mai niente a colazione.
He never eats anything for breakfast.

BUT if the negative pronoun is used before the verb, then **non** is not used:

Nessuno ha visitato il castello.
No one visited the castle.

9

Verbs ending in **-gliere** are irregular in the first-person singular and the third-person plural present tense, and they also have an irregular past participle:

scegliere (to choose)

present tense	present perfect
scelgo (I choose)	**ho scelto** (I have chosen)
scegli	
sceglie	
scegliamo	
scegliete	
scelgono (they choose)	

	"I"/"they" present	past participle
cogliere (to pick)	**colgo/colgono**	**colto**
sciogliere (to dissolve)	**sciolgo/sciolgono**	**sciolto**

Exercise 7

Complete these sentences using "stare per."
Example:
Non posso chiamarlo: ... uscire.→ Sta per uscire.

1 Non posso disturbarli: ... uscire.
2 Non posso mandarla a casa: ... dormire.
3 Non posso interromperli: ... finire.
4 Non posso invitarlo: ... andare in vacanza.
5 Non posso disturbarle: ... coricarsi.
6 Non posso portarlo qui a pranzo: ... andare al ristorante.
7 Non posso tenerli qui: ... partire.
8 Non posso ignorarli: ... salutarmi.
9 Non posso telefonarle: ... andare a letto.
10 Non posso chiamarli: ... prendere l'autobus.

Exercise 8

Read the following passage, checking any words you don't know in the vocabulary list at the end of the lesson, then translate it into English.

Lo Stato italiano

L'Italia è una repubblica dal 1946, l'anno in cui c'è stato il referendum per decidere se mantenere la monarchia o no. La monarchia ha perso e la casa di Savoia, che era la casa regnante, è andata in esilio.

La Costituzione, entrata in vigore nel 1948, stabilisce che il Presidente della Repubblica è Capo dello Stato ma non Capo del Governo; non è eletto dal popolo ma dai membri del Parlamento.

Il Capo del Governo è il Presidente del Consiglio, che insieme ai Ministri forma il Governo che deve essere approvato da tutte e due le Camere.

Il Parlamento è composto dalla Camera dei Deputati che ha 630 membri e dal Senato che ne ha 315. La Camera dei Deputati e il Senato sono eletti per cinque anni, il Presidente della Repubblica per sette anni.

Gli italiani votano a diciotto anni per la Camera (dei Deputati), ma possono votare per il Senato solo all'età di venticinque anni. Tuttavia, diversi partiti politici sono a favore della riduzione dell'età di voto a 16 anni.

9

Exercise 9

Now retranslate the previous passage back into Italian, correcting any mistakes against the original, then answer these questions with complete sentences:

1 L'Italia è diventata una Repubblica nel 1948?
2 Il Presidente della Repubblica è Capo del Governo?
3 Quanti deputati ci sono alla Camera?
4 A che età votano in Italia?
5 Quanti senatori ci sono al Senato?

9.10 SPELLING THINGS OUT

ACRONYMS

In Italian, most acronyms (such as **CIT** or **FIAT**) are pronounced as words. But some are pronounced as individual letters:

BBC   **la bi bi ci**

SPELLING

To pronounce these acronyms when speaking, or if you need to spell your name or another word, this is how to say the letters of the alphabet:

A	**a**	N	**enne**
B	**bi**	O	**o**
C	**ci**	P	**pi**
D	**di**	Q	**qu**
E	**e**	R	**erre**
F	**effe**	S	**esse**
G	**gi**	T	**ti**
H	**acca**	U	**u**
I	**i**	V	**vi, vu**
J	**i lunga**	W	**doppia vi, vu**
K	**kappa**	X	**ics**
L	**elle**	Y	**ipsilon**
M	**emme**	Z	**zeta**

9

Note that J, K, W, X, and Y are not part of the Italian alphabet, so are used only in loanwords.

When spelling out foreign words over the telephone in Italian, it is usual to give each letter followed by the name of a city:

"Root": **"erre" come Roma, "o" come Otranto, "o" come Otranto, "t" come Torino**

READING WEB AND EMAIL ADDRESSES

www	**vu vu vu**
@	**chiocciola**
gradi18@libero.it	**gradi diciotto chiocciola libero punto it**

Exercise 10

Translate the following sentences:

1 Give me (fam.) the suitcases, the train is coming in!

2 Not knowing anything, I didn't speak.

3 Not having a passport, I can't leave.

4 He can't come now because he is eating.

5 Tell me who it is! (fam.)

6 Go there immediately! (fam.)

7 I never choose the seat near the window.

8 It's so hot today, I'm going to faint.

9 I can't invite them; they are about to go out.

10 I did not know the people with whom you (form.) were staying.

9

Non li vada a trovare: stanno per uscire.
Quelli che lavorano con me sono tutti molto bravi.
Dammi del tu!
Mi ha chiamata proprio mentre stavo mangiando.
Non ho mai visto nessuno neanch'io.

alcuni	some, any
al di sotto	below
allievo/a	pupil, student, learner
altrimenti	otherwise
andare a trovare	to visit, to pay a visit to
anziano	old, elderly, senior
approvare	to approve
attento	careful
attualità (f.)	current affairs
aumento (m.)	increase
avanti	above, ahead, forward
avvocato / avvocatessa	lawyer
basso	low
Borsa (f.)	Stock Exchange
Camera (f.)	Chamber
capo/a	head, boss
Capo/a dello Stato	Head of State
castello (m.)	castle
che	who, whom, that, which
chi	the one/ones who
chiamare	to call
ciò che	what, that which
cogliere	to pick
Come mai?	How come?, Why?
Come no!	Yes, certainly!, Of course!
compagno/a	partner, companion
comunista (m. & f.)	communist
consistere	to consist
cosa (f.)	thing
costo (m.)	cost
cui	whom, which
dare del tu/del lei	to use tu/Lei
dare la mano	to shake hands

decisamente	definitely
dedicarsi	to devote oneself
delicato	delicate, tricky
democratico	democratic
deputato/a	Member of Parliament
dipendere	to depend
direttore / direttrice	director
discutere	to discuss
disturbare	to bother
diventare	to become
dollaro (m.)	dollar
domani	tomorrow
eccetto	except
eleggere	to elect
elezioni (f. pl.)	elections
elettronica (f.)	electronics
entrare in vigore	to become law
esilio (m.)	exile
esperto/a	expert
età (f.)	age
fabbricare	to manufacture
far vedere	to show
ferroviere/a	railroad worker
formare	to form
frutta (f.)	fruit
generale	general
gestire	to run (a business)
governo (m.)	government
ignorare	to ignore
il quale	who, whom, which, that
inflazione (f.)	inflation
Inghilterra (f.)	England
interrompere	to interrupt
invece	instead, on the contrary
invitare	to invite
Italia (f.)	Italy
liberale	liberal
lista (f.)	list
mantenere	to keep
media (f.)	average
membro (m. & f.)	member

9

Meno male!	Fortunately! Thank goodness!
mensa (f.)	refectory, canteen
mercato (m.)	market
mezzo (m.)	means (e.g., of transport)
mi pare	I think, it seems to me
momento (m.)	moment
monarchia (f.)	monarchy
notizie (f. pl.)	news
parente (m. & f.)	relative
parlamentare	parliamentary
Parlamento (m.)	Parliament
partita (f.)	match, game
partito (m.)	party (political party)
per cento	percent
per esempio	for example
personale	personal
piscina (f.)	swimming pool
popolo (m.)	people
portavoce (m. & f.)	spokesperson
presentare	to introduce
presidente (m. & f.)	chairperson, president
Presidente del Consiglio (m. & f.)	prime minister
presto	early
probabilmente	probably
questione (f.)	issue, question
quotidiano	daily
referendum (m.)	referendum
regionale	regional
regione (f.)	region
regnante	ruling
repubblica (f.)	republic
repubblicano/a	republican
restare	to stay, to remain
ricevere	to receive
riconoscere	to recognize
ricordarsi	to remember
riduzione (f.)	reduction, decrease
rivedere	to see again
salire	to climb, to go up
salutare	to greet

9

scegliere	to choose
sciogliere	to dissolve
sciopero (m.)	strike
seguire	to follow
Senato (m.)	Senate
senatore / senatrice	senator
sindacato (m.)	trade union
sistema (m.)	system
socialista (m. & f.)	socialist
società (f.)	company
spiegare	to explain
stabilire	to establish, to decide upon
stesso	same
stipendio (m.)	salary
suonare	to ring
svendita (f.)	sale
svenire	to faint
telefono (m.)	telephone
trasporto (m.)	transportation
treno (m.)	train
trovare	to find
tuttavia	however
ufficio (m.)	office
uguale	same, equal
vacanza (f.)	vacation, holiday
vecchio	old
verde	green
vita (f.)	life
votare	to vote
voto (m.)	vote

9

Week 10

You will learn:
- how to make small talk
- to talk about yourself, discuss your interests and your job
- to exchange comments on the weather

The grammar will include:
- the future tense
- irregular verbs in the future and conditional
- future perfect and past conditional
- reflexive pronouns **ci, vi, si** to translate "each other"/"one another"
- use of the prepositions **a, da, di**
- disjunctive pronouns (**me, te, lui, lei, noi, voi, loro, sé**)

CONVERSATION 1

Una gita in montagna

Tony and Jeff go on a coach trip to Monte Baldo, near Lake Garda. On the coach, Tony talks to Silvana, a young nurse whom they have just met.

SILVANA **Scusate, posso sedermi qui con voi?**

TONY **Certo, si accomodi.**

SILVANA **Grazie. Siete inglesi, vero?**

TONY **Sì, siamo di Londra. Il lago ci piace moltissimo e adesso vorremmo vedere un po' anche i monti vicini.**

SILVANA **A me la montagna piace anche più del lago. Vedrete che vista stupenda c'è dalla cima!**

TONY **Non vedo l'ora di arrivare al Monte Baldo! Quanto ci vorrà ancora?**

SILVANA **Mi hanno detto che arriveremo verso le undici. E poi dovremo fare una bella camminata di circa due ore.**

TONY **Noi non siamo abituati alle montagne in Inghilterra. Sarà difficile questa camminata fino alla cima?**

SILVANA **No, sono sicura di no. Neanch'io sono molto abituata alle camminate. Lavoro a**

Milano tutto l'anno e coi turni che faccio
ho poco tempo per gli svaghi!

TONY Proprio come noi. Lavoriamo in un
ospedale e spesso siamo di turno anche al
sabato e alla domenica.

SILVANA Ma guarda che coincidenza! Io faccio
l'infermiera al Policlinico di Milano.

TONY Siamo infermieri anche noi!

TRANSLATION 1

A trip to the mountains

SILVANA Excuse me, can I sit here with you?

TONY Sure, please do.

SILVANA Thank you. You're English, aren't you?

TONY Yes, we're from London. We like the lake
a lot, and now we'd like to see a bit of the
mountains nearby.

SILVANA I like the mountains even more than the lake.
You'll see what an amazing view there is from
the top!

TONY I can't wait to get to Monte Baldo! How much
longer will it take?

SILVANA They told me we'll arrive at around 11:00.
And then we'll have to do a good walk of
around two hours.

TONY We're not used to mountains in England. Will
it be hard, this walk to the top?

SILVANA No, I'm sure it won't. I'm not very used to
walking either. I work in Milan all year round,
and with the shifts I do, I have little time for
leisure activities!

TONY It's the same with us. We work in a hospital,
and we're often on duty even on Saturdays
and Sundays.

SILVANA What a coincidence! I'm a nurse at Milan
General Hospital.

TONY We are nurses, too!

10

Exercise 1

1 Dove vanno in gita Jeff, Tony e Silvana?
2 Dovranno camminare molto?
3 A che ora arriveranno al Monte Baldo?
4 Che cosa fa Silvana?
5 Dove lavorano tutti e tre?

10.1 THE FUTURE TENSE

The future tense is formed in a similar way to the conditional (see section 5.2), by removing the **-e** ending of the infinitive and adding **-o**, **-ai**, **-a**, **-emo**, **-ete**, **-anno**. In **-are** verbs, the **a** in the ending changes to **e**:

parlare	**prendere**	**finire**
(to speak)	(to take)	(to finish)
parlerò	**prenderò**	**finirò**
parlerai	**prenderai**	**finirai**
parlerà	**prenderà**	**finirà**
parleremo	**prenderemo**	**finiremo**
parlerete	**prenderete**	**finirete**
parleranno	**prenderanno**	**finiranno**

In Italian, the present tense is often used to express the immediate future, but to talk about a more distant or unknown future or to convey uncertainty, you should use the future tense. For example:

Vengono domani.
They are coming tomorrow. [I am sure of it.]

But

Verranno domani.
They will (probably) come tomorrow. [I am not sure.]
Chi vincerà le prossime elezioni?
Who will win the next elections? [The outcome is still unknown.]

10

Note that in the future tense, as with the conditional, a number of verbs have irregular stems:

1 Some verbs have a contracted stem or doubled letter:

andare	**andrò**	**andrei**
	I will go	I would go
avere	**avrò**	**avrei**
	I will have	I would have
bere	**berrò**	**berrei**
	I will drink	I would drink
cadere	**cadrò**	**cadrei**
	I will fall	I would fall
dovere	**dovrò**	**dovrei**
	I will have to	I would have to
essere	**sarò**	**sarei**
	I will be	I would be
potere	**potrò**	**potrei**
	I will be able to	I could
sapere	**saprò**	**saprei**
	I will know	I would know
tenere	**terrò**	**terrei**
	I will keep	I would keep
vedere	**vedrò**	**vedrei**
	I will see	I would see
venire	**verrò**	**verrei**
	I will come	I would come
vivere	**vivrò**	**vivrei**
	I will live	I would live

2 Verbs ending in **-care** and **-gare** insert an **h** after the **c** or **g** of the stem (this is done to keep the hard "c" and "g" sounds):

cercare	**cercherò**	**cercherei**
	I will seek	I would seek

10

pagare	pagherò	pagherei
	I will pay	I would pay

3 Verbs ending in **-ciare**, **-giare**, **-sciare** drop the final **i** of the stem:

cominciare	comincerò	comincerei
	I will start	I would start
mangiare	mangerò	mangerei
	I will eat	I would eat
lasciare	lascerò	lascerei
	I will leave	I would leave

4 Some verbs ending in **-are** keep the **a** vowel of the stem:

dare	darò	darei
	I will give	I would give
fare	farò	farei
	I will do	I would do
stare	starò	starei
	I will stay	I would stay

10

Exercise 2

Answer these questions using the expression "prima o poi" (sooner or later) and the future tense.

Example:
Vuole cominciare oggi?→ Prima o poi comincerò.

1 Vuole venire oggi?

2 Vuole pagare oggi?

3 Vuole ballare oggi?

4 Vuole andare oggi?

5 Vuole giocare oggi?

6 Vuole scegliere oggi?

7 Vuole finire oggi?

8 Vuole ordinare oggi?

9 Vuole ritornare oggi?

10 Vuole studiare oggi?

Exercise 3

Change these sentences by adding magari ("perhaps," "maybe") and using the future tense.

Example:
Vado da sola.→ Magari andrò da sola.
I am going alone.→ Perhaps I'll go alone.

1 Vengono a piedi.

2 Possiamo dormire in tenda.

3 Portate voi qualcosa da mangiare.

4 Usciamo più tardi.

5 Fa più bella figura.

6 Non gli danno la mancia.

7 Ci aspettano all'altra fermata.

8 Canto un'altra aria.

9 Paghi tutto insieme.

10 Gestisce lui il ristorante.

10

10.3 FUTURE PERFECT AND PAST CONDITIONAL

The future perfect ("I will have done") and the past conditional in Italian ("I would have done") are formed with the future or conditional of **avere** or **essere** plus the past participle of the main verb.

future perfect

avrò	parlato	sarò	andato/a
avrai		sarai	
avrà		sarà	
avremo		saremo	andati/e
avrete		sarete	
avranno		saranno	

past conditional

avrei	parlato	sarei	andato/a
avresti		saresti	
avrebbe		sarebbe	
avremmo		saremmo	andati/e
avreste		sareste	
avrebbero		sarebbero	

Fra due ore saranno arrivati sulla cima.
In two hours, they will have arrived at the top.

Note that the future perfect is also used to express probability in the past:

Non hai passato l'esame? Avrai studiato ben poco!
Haven't you passed the exam? You must have ("will have") studied very little!

The past conditional in Italian is used in a conditional clause when the past tense is used in the main clause of the sentence:

Mi ha detto che sarebbe venuto.
He told me that he would ("would have") come.

10

Il lavoro

Tony and Jeff have made friends with Silvana and are now discussing jobs and interests with her. Tony does all the talking because Jeff doesn't speak much Italian.

SILVANA **Da quanto tempo lavorate in ospedale?**
TONY **Io da tre anni, ma Jeff da due. A me il lavoro piace, e a te?**
SILVANA **Sì, mi piace, ma è un po' duro. Lavoro quattro o anche cinque turni di dodici ore alla settimana!**
TONY **Per noi è difficile perché non abbiamo sempre gli stessi turni e così certe settimane ci vediamo a malapena.**
SILVANA **Vivete insieme?**
TONY **Sì, da un anno. Purtroppo noi abbiamo poco tempo per altri interessi. E tu?**
SILVANA **Mi piace andare a cavallo, ma costa caro a Milano. Mi piace anche andare al cinema.**
TONY **Io faccio collezione di francobolli, ma a Jeff piacciono cose più artistiche. Va a teatro e al cinema come te.**

Work

SILVANA How long have you both been working at the hospital?
TONY Me, for three years, but Jeff for two. I like my job, do you?
SILVANA Yes, I do, but it's a little hard. I work four or even five 12-hour shifts per week.
TONY For us, it's difficult because we don't always have the same shifts, so some weeks we hardly see each other.

10

SILVANA	Do you live together?
TONY	Yes, we've lived together for a year. Unfortunately, we don't have much time for other interests. And you?
SILVANA	I enjoy riding, but it's expensive in Milan. I like going to the movies, too.
TONY	I collect stamps, but Jeff likes more artistic things. He goes to the theater and the movies, like you.

Exercise 4

Read and listen to Conversation 2, then answer the following questions:

1 Da quanto tempo lavorano Tony e Jeff in ospedale?
2 Quanti turni fa Silvana alla settimana?
3 Perché Tony e Jeff si vedono a malapena certe settimane?
4 A Silvana piace andare a cavallo?
5 Che cosa piace a Tony?

10.4 EACH OTHER / ONE ANOTHER

In Italian, you use the reflexive pronouns **ci, vi, si** to translate "each other" or "one another":

Ci conosciamo.
We know each other.
Si parlano.
They speak to one another.
Vi telefonate spesso?
Do you phone each other often?
Si danno del tu.
They use **tu** with each other.

10

Here is a summary of the uses of the prepositions **a**, **da**, and **di**, most of which you have already seen.

THE PREPOSITION **A**

The preposition **a** is used:

1 To translate the English "to":

Parlo a Maria.
I'm speaking to Maria.
Vado a Roma.
I'm going to Rome.

2 To translate the English "at" or "in" to indicate place (except with names of countries):

Abito a Milano.
I live in Milan.
Sto a casa.
I'm staying at home.

BUT with names of countries you use **in**:

Vivo in Italia.
I live in Italy.

3 To translate the English "at" with expressions of time:

Arrivo alle due.
I'm arriving at two o'clock.
a notte fonda
at nightfall

10

4 To express means or manner:

Giochiamo a tennis.
We play tennis.
Vado a piedi.
I'm going on foot.
Lavo tutto a mano.
I wash everything by hand.

5 With expressions of distance and price:

Costa tre euro al chilo.
It costs 3 euros a kilo.
Milano è a trecento chilometri da Venezia.
Milan is 300 km from Venice.

6 With expressions that describe "style":

una trota alla griglia
a grilled trout
un vestito a righe
a striped dress

7 With other prepositions such as: **vicino a** (near), **insieme a** (together with), **in cima a** (on top of), **davanti a** (in front of), **fino a** (as far as), **di fronte a** (opposite), **in mezzo a** (in the middle of), etc.

THE PREPOSITION **DA**
The preposition **da** is used:

1 To translate the English "from":

Il treno parte da Genova.
The train is leaving from Genoa.
Sono lontano da casa.
I am far from home.

2 To translate the English "by":

Vivo da sola.
I live by myself.
È curato dal medico.
He is cured by the doctor.

3 To translate the English "as" in time expressions:

da bambina
as a child
da giovane
as a young person

4 To translate the English "for" to express uninterrupted time:

Abito a Roma da due mesi.
I have lived in Rome for two months.
Studio da tre mesi.
I have been studying for three months.
È morto da un anno.
He has been dead a year.

Note that in these expressions, you must use the present tense in Italian, not the present perfect.

5 To translate the English "to" or "at the house/office/shop of":

Vado dal giornalaio.
I am going to the newsdealer.
Vieni da me?
Are you coming to my place?
Ti fermi da Mario?
Are you staying at Mario's?

10

6 To describe inherent physical characteristics or quality:

una tazza da tè
a tea cup
un francobollo da quaranta centesimi
a 40-cent stamp
È roba da pazzi!
It's sheer lunacy!

7 To express purpose before an infinitive:

Ho molto da fare.
I have a lot to do.
Vorrei qualcosa da leggere.
I'd like something to read.

THE PREPOSITION DI

The preposition **di** is used:

1 To translate the English "of" or "'s" (see Week 2):

un albergo pieno di turisti
a hotel full of tourists
la divisa di un infermiere
a nurse's uniform

2 To indicate origin:

Sono di Verona.
I am from [i.e., was born in] Verona.

3 With comparatives (see Week 8):

Il Monte Bianco è più alto del Monte Baldo.
Mont Blanc is higher than Monte Baldo.

10

4 To describe the material of which something is made:

una camicia di cotone
a cotton shirt
una scatola di legno
a wooden box

5 In certain idiomatic expressions:

Mi pare di sì.	I think so.
Dice di no.	He says no.
niente di nuovo	nothing new

6 With other prepositions, such as **a fianco di** (at the side of), **prima di** (before), **a causa di** (because of), etc.

Exercise 5

Complete the following questions with the correct preposition.

Example:
La banca è davanti ... la farmacia.→ La banca è davanti alla farmacia. (The bank is in front of the pharmacy.)

1 Giovanni mi ha detto ... sì.

2 Domani forse andremo ... Maria.

3 Ho comprato una camicia ... seta.

4 Lavora all'ospedale ... un anno.

5 Silvana è ... Milano.

6 Il giornalaio è di fronte ... la banca.

7 Oggi giochiamo ... calcio.

8 L'autobus arriva ... le due.

9 Hai molto ... fare?

10 Il suo ufficio è ... duecento metri ... biblioteca.

10

CONVERSATION 3

Una gita a Cortina / A trip to Cortina

Peter and Luisa are planning a skiing vacation.

PETER **Hai gli scarponi da sci?**

LUISA **No, pensavo di prenderli a noleggio, con gli sci.**

PETER **Io li ho presi in prestito da Gianni. Ma c'è un negozio che li dà a nolo.**

LUISA **Dov'è? È quello dietro all'ostello?**

PETER **No, è di fianco alla posta. Ma hai visto che piove?**

LUISA **Allora non possiamo sciare se fa così brutto tempo.**

PETER **Magari a Cortina ci sarà il sole, perché non ci andiamo lo stesso?**

LUISA **D'accordo, se fa brutto tempo anche lì, ci fermeremo in quel bel ristorante sopra alla funivia.**

PETER **Prendo la macchina dal garage e ci troviamo di fronte a casa tua.**

TRANSLATION 3

PETER Do you have ski boots?

LUISA No, I was thinking of renting them, with the skis.

PETER I borrowed them from Gianni. But there's a shop that rents them out.

LUISA Where is it? Is it the one behind the hostel?

PETER No, it's next to the post office. But have you noticed that it's raining?

LUISA Then we can't ski if the weather is so bad.

PETER Maybe in Cortina it will be sunny; why don't we go all the same?

LUISA All right, if the weather is bad there, we can stop at that nice restaurant at the top of the cable car.

PETER I'll get the car from the garage, and we'll meet in front of your house.

10

Exercise 6

Read and listen to Conversation 3, then answer the following questions:

1 Da chi ha preso in prestito gli scarponi Peter?
2 Dove danno sci a nolo?
3 Che tempo fa adesso?
4 Se fa brutto tempo a Cortina cosa faranno?
5 Dove si trovano Peter e Luisa?

10.6 DISJUNCTIVE PRONOUNS

These are stressed pronouns that are used for emphasis or in isolation. They are:

me	me
te	you (fam. sing.)
lei	her
Lei	you (formal sing.)
lui	him
noi	us
voi	you (pl.)
loro	them
sé	himself/herself/themselves/oneself

They are used:

1 After a preposition:

Vado con lui.
I am going with him.
Lavora per sé.
He/She works for himself/herself.

2 In exclamations:

Povera me!	Poor me!
Beati voi!	Lucky you!

10

3 In comparisons:

Sono più vecchio di te.
I am older than you.

4 Instead of direct or indirect object pronouns in order to convey emphasis or to avoid ambiguity when there are two objects:

Parla a me non a voi.
He is speaking to me, not to you.
Carlo chiama me, non te.
Charles is calling me, not you.
A me il teatro non piace.
As for me, I don't like the theater.
Imposterà lui la lettera.
He (emphatic) will post the letter.

10

Exercise 7

Change the words in brackets into the appropriate disjunctive (stressed) pronouns.

Examples:

Parlo a [Maria] non a [Enzo].→ Parlo a lei non a lui.
[Mi] telefona davvero?→ Telefona davvero a me?

1 [Gli] scriverai davvero?
2 Guardo [il bambino] non [la madre].
3 [Ci] parla, ma non a nessun altro.
4 Siete sicuri che [vi] scriverà?
5 C'è molta gente prima di [Mario].
6 [Le] manderai solo un regalo?
7 Parlano spesso di [Carlo e Marina].
8 Fa tutto da [solo].
9 Andiamo a cavallo con [le ragazze].
10 [Mi] invitano proprio?

Exercise 8

Translate the following sentences:

1 We will write to you (pl.) soon.
2 We have known each other for three years.
3 They bought a silk tie for their father.
4 I work as a nurse in Florence.
5 Do you (fam.) have a lot to do?
6 I want to see you (fam.), not your girlfriend!
7 I will start studying next week.
8 They went to Maria's for dinner.
9 Lucky you (form.)!
10 The hospital is opposite the bank.

10

Giocheremo a tennis.
Non avranno voluto restare da lei.
Il negozio è dietro alla banca.
Forse domani farà bel tempo.

VOCABULARY

a causa di	because of
a fianco di	at the side of, next to, alongside
a malapena	hardly
aiuto (m.)	help
alto	high, tall
aria (f.)	air, tune
artistico	artistic
assegno (m.)	check
beato/a/i/e	lucky (in exclamations), blessed
biblioteca (f.)	library
blusa (f.)	blouse
camminata (f.)	walk
cantare	to sing
cavallo (m.)	horse
andare a cavallo	to go horseback riding
cercare	to look for, to seek
chilometro (m.)	kilometer
cinema (m.)	cinema, movies
circa	about, approximately
coincidenza (f.)	coincidence
collezione (f.)	collection
cotone (m.)	cotton
curare	to cure
dietro a	behind
di fronte a	in front of, opposite
di turno	on duty
divisa (f.)	uniform
duro	hard
essere abituato a	to be used to
fare bella figura	to look good, to impress
fare conoscenza	to get acquainted
farmacia (f.)	pharmacy
fermata (f.)	stop

10

fino a	as far as
francobollo (m.)	stamp
funivia (f.)	cable car
gente (f.)	people
gita (f.)	trip, excursion
guida (f.)	guide
in cima a	on top of
infermiere/a	nurse
insieme a	together with
legno (m.)	wood
lì	there
magari	perhaps, maybe
medico/a	doctor
montagna (f.)	mountain
monte (m.)	mount, mountain
morire	to die
morto	dead
noleggio, nolo (m.)	rental, hire
non veder l'ora di	to look forward to
ordinare	to order, to put in order
pazzo	mad, crazy, insane
piedi (m. pl.)	feet
Policlinico	General Hospital
posta (f.)	mail, post, post office
povero	poor
prendere in prestito	to borrow
prestare	to lend
prestito (m.)	loan
prima di	before
riga (f.)	stripe, line
scarponi (m. pl.)	boots
scatola (f.)	box
sci (m. pl.)	skis
sciare	to ski
seta (f.)	silk
svago (m.)	pastime, leisure, recreation
turno (m.)	duty, shift
ufficio postale (m.)	post office

10

Key to Exercises

In this key, we haven't included the underlined vowel to indicate where the word stress lies when this is not on the second-to-last syllable.

Week 1

Exercise 1: 1 Sì, è americana. 2 No, è italiano. 3 Sì, è libera. 4 Sì, è americano. 5 Sì, è solo per oggi. 6 Sì, è italiano. 7 No, è americana. 8 Sì, è italiano. 9 Sì, è singola. 10 No, è singola.

Exercise 2: 1 Non sono di Verona. 2 Sandro Bianchi non ha una bella casa. 3 L'albergo non è pieno. 4 La signorina non lavora in un albergo. 5 Non parlate bene l'italiano?

Exercise 3: 1 Questo è lo zoo. 2 Parliamo bene l'italiano. 3 Il marito di Mary è inglese. 4 Rita è la moglie di Sandro. 5 Ascolto l'opera alla Scala. 6 La signora è italiana. 7 L'albergo è molto comodo. 8 Questa è la camera singola. 9 Ecco la chiave. 10 Ecco il passaporto.

Exercise 4: 1 No, è americano. 2 Si chiama Mary. 3 Abita a Venezia. 4 Sono di Milano. 5 Sandro lavora a Venezia. 6 Sì, lavora in un albergo. 7 Sì, è giornalista. 8 No, lavora nel centro di New York. 9 Mary è insegnante. 10 Sì, Mary e John abitano in una casa con giardino.

Exercise 5: 1 Abito a Milano. 2 Lavora a Venezia? 3 Dove abita? 4 Sono giornalista. 5 Rita Rossi parla italiano. 6 Abitiamo a Pavia e lavoriamo a Milano. 7 New York City è bella. 8 Avete il passaporto americano? 9 Di dove siete? 10 Sono americano/a.

Week 2

Exercise 1: 1 No, è un po' piccola. 2 È in fondo al corridoio a destra. 3 Sì. 4 Nello sgabuzzino. 5 È vicino alla cucina.

Exercise 2: 1 Queste sono le mie camere. 2 I bagni sono occupati. 3 Lavoriamo per la nostra compagnia.

4 Gli studenti americani studiano molto. 5 Le sue valigie sono vuote. 6 I pasti cominciano dopo le nove. 7 I nostri pensionanti parlano bene le lingue. 8 Le signore arrivano con le figlie. 9 Se le porte sono aperte noi entriamo. 10 Gli appartamenti al primo piano sono spaziosi.

Exercise 3: 1 Ha tre camere da letto. 2 È al quarto piano. 3 Va a casa di Maria. 4 No, vive in periferia. 5 Sì, c'è la metropolitana vicino.

Exercise 4:
... abito in periferia.
... c'è la metropolitana vicino.
... una casa piccola con un giardino grande.
... una cucina grande.
... due camere da letto e un bagno.
... è abbastanza vicino.

Exercise 5: 1 vive 2 dormono 3 prendiamo 4 sentite 5 apri 6 vedete 7 vestono 8 sentite 9 mette 10 conosciamo

Exercise 6: 1 i suoi 2 Il suo 3 la loro 4 i vostri 5 i miei 6 tua 7 la nostra 8 mio 9 le Sue 10 le vostre

Exercise 7: 1 Sì, ha bambini. 2 No. L'affitto del garage è extra. 3 No. Non desidera avere la biancheria. 4 È in Piazza Indipendenza. 5 Sì, c'è tutto il necessario.

Exercise 8: 1 È del signor Rossi. 2 È degli studenti. 3 È del mio amico. 4 È della signora Rossi. 5 È dei bambini.

Exercise 9: 1 allo 2 al 3 alla 4 ai 5 alle 6 all' 7 agli

Exercise 10: 1 Troviamo gli appartamenti ammobiliati sui giornali. 2 Le figlie delle signore vivono con i loro ragazzi. 3 Non vediamo la differenza tra queste case e le altre. 4 Le chiavi delle porte sono dalle portinaie. 5 Gli inquilini prendono le cartoline dalle cassette delle lettere.

Exercise 11: 1 Metto la mia macchina in garage. 2 Parto per l'ufficio da solo. 3 Scrivi a tua sorella oggi?/Scrive a Sua sorella oggi? 4 Suo fratello vive qui? 5 Sente molto rumore nella strada affollata.

Exercise 12: 1 Maria vive con suo padre a Roma. 2 Il mio appartamento è vicino al centro di Milano. 3 Di chi è questa camera? È dei bambini. 4 La loro cucina è piccola. 5 Dove abitate, in un appartamento o in una casa?

Week 3

Exercise 1: 1 Va all'Ufficio del Turismo. 2 Desidera una cartina di Roma. 3 Dal tabaccaio o dal giornalaio.
4 Per settantacinque minuti.

Exercise 2: 1 Quella cartina è gratis. 2 Quell'autobus è affollato. 3 Quel treno è veloce. 4 Quello scompartimento è riservato. 5 Partite con quegli amici di Emma? 6 Porti quelle valigie in stazione? 7 Quei biglietti sono di andata e ritorno. 8 Quegli orari non sono giusti. 9 Parti con quell'aereo? 10 Sono liberi quei posti?

Exercise 3: 1 Questo è il mio posto. 2 Questi biglietti sono validi per tre ore. 3 Questi sono i miei ospiti italiani. 4 Prendiamo quel treno. 5 È quella la fermata? 6 Quei bambini sono inglesi. 7 Viaggiamo su quell'autobus. 8 Quelle sono le mie valigie. 9 Quello sportello è aperto. 10 Questa è la stazione.

Exercise 4: 1 Va in Piazza Navona. 2 Sono le undici e mezzo. 3 A mezzogiorno. 4 Ci vuole circa un quarto d'ora. 5 Il venticinque.

Exercise 5: 1 Sono le due e mezzo. 2 Sono le tre. 3 Sono le ventuno. 4 Sono le dodici e quindici/È mezzogiorno e un quarto. 5 È mezzanotte/Sono le ventiquattro. 6 Sono le quattro e tre quarti/Sono le cinque meno un quarto. 7 Sono le otto e trentacinque.

8 È l'una e mezzo. 9 Sono le due e cinquanta/Sono le tre meno dieci. 10 Sono le sette e dieci.

Exercise 6: 1 A che ora parte l'autobus? Alle sei. 2 A che ora parte l'aereo? Alle sette e trenta. 3 A che ora parte il treno? Alle ventidue e trenta. 4 A che ora arriva il treno? Alle diciassette e venticinque. 5 A che ora arriva l'autobus? Alle tredici e quindici.

Exercise 7: 1 È andato alla stazione. 2 Perché il treno è partito in ritardo. 3 È partita da Siena. 4 Ha prenotato il ristorante. 5 Ha preparato la camera per Luisa.

Exercise 8: 1 Ieri Mario è arrivato alle tre. 2 Ieri il treno è partito alle nove. 3 Ieri l'autobus è arrivato in ritardo. 4 Ieri Maria è partita con il treno. 5 Ieri i signori Bianchi sono arrivati alle due. 6 Ieri le valigie sono cadute per terra. 7 Ieri la passeggera è andata in macchina. 8 Ieri noi siamo partite all'una. 9 Ieri voi siete andati in treno? 10 Ieri i viaggiatori sono andati a prendere il taxi.

Exercise 9: 1 Un'ora fa ho guidato la macchina. 2 Un'ora fa ho mangiato il pranzo. 3 Un'ora fa Maria ha preparato la colazione. 4 Un'ora fa abbiamo venduto la nostra macchina. 5 Un'ora fa hanno comprato i biglietti. 6 Un'ora fa i passeggeri hanno guardato l'orario. 7 Un'ora fa hai sentito questo rumore? 8 Un'ora fa abbiamo finito il pranzo. 9 Un'ora fa abbiamo prenotato il ristorante. 10 Un'ora fa hanno portato le valigie sul treno.

Exercise 10:
– Benissimo, grazie. Ma l'aereo è partito in ritardo da Roma. Così sono arrivato a Cagliari in ritardo.
– Alle dieci e tre quarti, ma sono partito da casa alle sette.
– No, ho preso una macchina a noleggio.
– Sì, ma ho deciso di prendere la macchina a noleggio per una settimana.
– Non ho visto il centro. Vorrei andare in tutti i posti famosi.

Exercise 11: Oggi Francesca è tornata dalla Sardegna. È arrivata in aereo, l'aereo ha fatto scalo ad Alghero e il volo è durato tre ore. È stata a Cagliari poi ha preso una macchina a noleggio ed è andata a Nuoro per due giorni, ma non ha avuto molto tempo per vedere la città. Ha firmato il contratto per il nuovo albergo. Ha visto anche il nuovo direttore. Ha fatto molto, ma la prossima volta desidera restare più a lungo.

Week 4

Exercise 1: 1 Rita vuole affittare un appartamento. 2 Non posso guardare questa lista? 3 Vorrei prenotare una camera. 4 Non possiamo pagare molto. 5 Dobbiamo partire alle nove. 6 Volete andare al campeggio? 7 Possono venire oggi. 8 Deve pagare di più. 9 Vuole stare in una pensione? 10 Se posso voglio stare a Venezia per tre giorni.

Exercise 2: 1 Devo andare più tardi. 2 Devo aspettare alla stazione. 3 Devo vedere la mia padrona di casa. 4 Voglio venire alle tre. 5 Voglio restare in albergo. 6 Voglio vedere i miei amici. 7 Posso venire a mezzogiorno. 8 Posso restare al campeggio. 9 Posso invitare una collega. 10 Posso pagare stasera.

Exercise 3: 1 Vuole una casetta in campagna. 2 Preferisce abitare in campagna. 3 Sì, può trovare un appartamento non restaurato. 4 Sì, ma deve telefonare al mattino. 5 Sì, c'è l'acqua.

Exercise 4: 1 Sì, scriva pure! 2 Sì, cominci pure! 3 Sì, finisca pure! 4 Sì, mangi pure! 5 Sì, pulisca pure! 6 Sì, chiuda pure! 7 Sì, serva pure! 8 Sì, guardi pure! 9 Sì, parta pure! 10 Sì, entri pure!

Exercise 5: 1 Sì, scrivi pure! 2 Sì, comincia pure! 3 Sì, finisci pure! 4 Sì, mangia pure! 5 Sì, pulisci pure! 6 Sì, chiudi pure! 7 Sì, servi pure! 8 Sì, guarda pure! 9 Sì, parti pure! 10 Sì, entra pure!

Exercise 6: 1 Scusate, dobbiamo scrivere? Sì, scrivete pure! 2 Scusate, dobbiamo cominciare? Sì, cominciate pure! 3 Scusate, dobbiamo finire? Sì, finite pure! 4 Scusate, dobbiamo mangiare? Sì, mangiate pure! 5 Scusate, dobbiamo pulire? Sì, pulite pure! 6 Scusate, dobbiamo chiudere? Sì, chiudete pure! 7 Scusate, dobbiamo servire? Sì, servite pure! 8 Scusate, dobbiamo guardare? Sì, guardate pure! 9 Scusate, dobbiamo partire? Sì, partite pure! 10 Scusate, dobbiamo entrare? Sì, entrate pure!

Exercise 7: 1 Signora, non chiuda la finestra, per favore! 2 Mario, non portare la mia valigia, per favore! 3 Piero non guardare la televisione, per favore! 4 Signora, non prenda la chiave, per favore! 5 Maria, non prendere la chiave, per favore! 6 Ragazzi, non guardate questo salotto, per favore! 7 Ragazze, non prendete questa strada, per favore! 8 Signor Rossi, non guardi là per favore. 9 Non scendiamo insieme le scale! 10 Sandro, non prendere l'ombrello!

Exercise 8: 1 Sì, certo, vada pure! 2 Sì, certo, stia pure! 3 Sì, certo, faccia pure! 4 Sì, certo, dia pure! 5 Sì, certo, tenga pure! 6 Sì, certo, venga pure! 7 Sì, certo, finisca pure! 8 Sì, certo, pulisca pure! 9 Sì, certo, beva pure! 10 Sì, certo, legga pure!

Exercise 9: 1 Oggi è martedì. 2 È il trentun gennaio duemilaventuno. 3 Costa trecentomila euro. 4 È agosto. 5 Costano un euro. 6 Ha seicentomila abitanti. 7 È finita nel millenovecentoquaranta-cinque. 8 È nata nel millenovecentotrentadue. 9 Costa sei euro e sessantacinque (centesimi). 10 Costa centoventi euro.

Exercise 10: 1 Ci sono le docce, i gabinetti, la cucina e la lavanderia. 2 No, hanno la roulotte. 3 No, non hanno prenotato il posto. 4 Sì, c'è un supermercato al campeggio.

Exercise 11: 1 Devono prenotare la stanza prima di agosto. 2 Non sono andati in Italia nel duemilaventuno. 3 Preferiamo un appartamento al pianterreno. 4 Vogliono comprare una casa in campagna. 5 Possiamo guardare il rustico la settimana prossima? 6 L'appuntamento è per venerdì prossimo alle quindici. 7 L'agenzia immobiliare può fissare una visita al mattino. 8 Vorrei venire, ma oggi devo stare a casa. 9 Mi dispiace, ma vorrei una camera con bagno. 10 Non compri questa casa, è troppo lontano dal centro.

Week 5

Exercise 1: 1 No, non lo prende. 2 Lo offre la signora Fazzini. 3 La offre il signor White. 4 Sì, lo prende. 5 Sì, le mangiano.

Exercise 2: 1 Sì, la guardo spesso. 2 Sì, le compro spesso. 3 Sì, li invito spesso. 4 Sì, lo bevo spesso. 5 Sì, lo prendo spesso. 6 Sì, la porto spesso. 7 Sì, le mangio spesso. 8 Sì, li bevo spesso. 9 Sì, li bevo spesso. 10 Sì, la invito [l'invito] spesso.

Exercise 3: 1 Le parlo adesso. 2 Gli parlo adesso. 3 Gli telefono adesso. 4 Le rispondo adesso. 5 Gli scrivo [scrivo loro] adesso. 6 Gli scrivo [scrivo loro] adesso. 7 Gli rispondo [rispondo loro] adesso. 8 Gli telefono adesso. 9 Gli parlo [parlo loro] adesso. 10 Le scrivo adesso.

Exercise 4: 1 Le dà il numero. 2 Non lo sento. 3 Il signor Forti la legge. 4 La signora le prende. 5 Li compriamo qui. 6 Gli offro [offro loro] l'aperitivo. 7 Gli telefono. 8 Le scrivete? 9 Che cosa gli portate? 10 Il signor Rossi non la lascia.

Exercise 5: 1 Beve un caffè corretto. 2 No, beve un caffè corretto. 3 È un posto dove si beve soprattutto il vino. 4 Tony offre da bere. 5 Lo beve Jeff.

Exercise 6: 1 Sì, dovremmo partire ma abbiamo cambiato idea. 2 Sì, dovrei andare ma non ho la macchina. 3 Sì, potrei venire ma più tardi. 4 Sì, potremmo accompagnarlo in macchina. 5 Sì, vorrei telefonare ma non ho il tempo. 6 Sì, vorremmo viaggiare ma non da soli. 7 No, vorrei un cappuccino. 8 No, vorremmo mangiare alle due. 9 No, potrei venire in bicicletta. 10 Sì, dovremmo restare per la cena.

Exercise 7: 1 Sì, lo compri! 2 Sì, la mangi! 3 Sì, le parli! 4 Sì, li venda! 5 Sì, le prenoti! 6 Sì, la faccia! 7 Sì, la dia! 8 Sì, li porti! 9 Sì, gli telefoni! 10 Sì, lo prenda!

Exercise 8: 1 Sì, compralo! No, non comprarlo! 2 Sì, mangiala! No, non mangiarla!

3 Sì, parlale! No, non parlarle! 4 Sì, vendili! No, non venderli! 5 Sì, prenotale! No, non prenotarle! 6 Sì, falla! No, non farla! 7 Sì, dalla! No, non darla! 8 Sì, portali! No, non portarli! 9 Sì, telefonagli! No, non telefonargli! 10 Sì, prendilo! No, non prenderlo!

Exercise 9: 1 può 2 so 3 sai 4 so 5 possiamo 6 sa 7 sa 8 posso 9 possono 10 sa

Exercise 10: 1 Sì, mi piace moltissimo. 2 Sì, mi piacciono moltissimo. 3 Sì, mi piace moltissimo. 4 Sì, mi piace moltissimo. 5 Sì, mi piacciono moltissimo. 6 No, non mi piacciono. 7 No, non mi piace. 8 No, non mi piacciono. 9 No, non mi piace. 10 No, non mi piacciono.

Exercise 11: 1 L'amico di Luigi, perché è vegetariano. 2 Ci sono l'insalata, le patate fritte, i finocchi, verdure fresche. 3 No, li prende solo la signora. 4 No, lo ordina rosso. 5 No, c'è anche la trota. 6 Tre persone la mangiano.

Exercise 12: 1 Non ci piace viaggiare in treno. 2 Ti piacciono le patate fritte? 3 Per favore dia questa chiave alla signora Rossi. 4 Andresti da solo? 5 Maria, non prendere la mia macchina, prendi la tua. 6 Gli abbiamo dato tutte le informazioni necessarie. 7 Vi posso offrire qualcosa da bere? 8 Da quanto [tempo] studiate l'italiano? 9 Comprerebbero l'appartamento, ma costa quattrocentomila euro. 10 Siamo andati a pranzo da Tony.

Week 6

Exercise 1: 1 La fa dal droghiere. 2 Ne compra più di due etti. 3 Preferisce il reggiano. 4 Ne compra due.

Exercise 2: 1 Ne vorrei un litro. 2 Ne vorrei un chilo e mezzo. 3 Ne vorrei una sola. 4 Ne vorrei due etti. 5 Ne vorrei due chili. 6 Ne ho una. 7 Ne ho quattro. 8 Non ne ho molte. 9 Ne ho pochi. 10 Non ne ho.

Exercise 3: 1 Sì, li ho invitati. 2 Sì, l'ho visitata.

3 Sì l'ho visitato. 4 Sì, li ho portati. 5 Sì, le ho mangiate. 6 Sì, l'abbiamo invitata. 7 Sì, l'abbiamo guardato. 8 Sì, le abbiamo comprate. 9 Sì, l'abbiamo presa. 10 Sì, l'abbiamo visto.

Exercise 4: 1 Vuole il quarantasei. 2 Lo preferisce blu. 3 Sono al terzo piano. 4 Porta il quarantadue. 5 Li compra per gli amici americani.

Exercise 5: 1 Sì, glieli porto. 2 Sì, gliela scrivo. 3 Sì, glielo do. 4 Sì, glieli do. 5 Sì, glielo porto. 6 Sì, gliele scrivo. 7 Sì, gliela compro. 8 Sì, glieli compro. 9 Sì, glielo vendo. 10 Sì, gliela vendo.

Exercise 6: 1 Hai portato i panini ai ragazzi? Sì, glieli ho portati. 2 Hai scritto la lettera a Maria? Sì, gliel'ho scritta. 3 Hai dato il conto alla signora? Sì, gliel'ho dato. 4 Hai dato i soldi alla signora? Sì, glieli ho dati. 5 Hai portato il vestito al signor Bianchi? Sì, gliel'ho portato. 6 Hai scritto le lettere a tutti? Sì, gliele ho scritte. 7 Hai comprato la pasta per gli ospiti? Si, gliel'ho comprata. 8 Hai comprato i grissini per Maria? Si, glieli ho comprati. 9 Hai venduto l'appartamento a questi signori? Si, gliel'ho venduto. 10 Hai venduto la casa a questi signori? Sì, gliel'ho venduta.

Exercise 7: 1 Me l'ha consigliato un'amica. 2 Me l'ha dato il poliziotto. 3 Me l'ha portata il facchino. 4 Me l'ha riparato l'orologiaio. 5 Me li ha mandati un amico. 6 Ce l'ha portato il cameriere. 7 Ce le ha vendute la commessa. 8 Ce li ha comprati nostra figlia. 9 Ce l'ha prenotato l'agenzia. 10 Ce l'ha data l'impiegata.

Exercise 8: 1 Sì, me lo porti pure. 2 Sì, me li mandi pure. 3 Sì, me le regali pure. 4 Sì, me la scriva pure. 5 Sì, me lo prenoti pure.

Exercise 9: 1 Sì, preparamela pure! 2 Sì, mandamele pure! 3 Sì, comprameli pure! 4 Sì, scrivimelo pure! 5 Sì, prendimela pure!

Exercise 10: 1 L'ha messa dentro il Bancomat. 2 C'è scritto che ha aspettato troppo. 3 Sì, è chiusa. 4 No, non li ha persi. 5 Perché non è riuscito a ritirare i soldi dal Bancomat.

Exercise 11: 1 Il reparto calzature è al decimo piano.
2 Questa è la sesta settimana. 3 Il primo maggio è una festa nazionale in Italia. 4 Viviamo nel ventunesimo secolo.
5 Prenda la quarta via alla Sua sinistra.

Exercise 12: Ieri Tony e Luisa sono andati alla Rinascente per comprare due regali: uno per la madre di Tony e l'altro per quella di Luisa. Luisa è andata al pianterreno, al reparto accessori, e ha comprato una borsetta di pelle. Tony è andato a dare un'occhiata al reparto casalinghi al sesto piano. Ha guardato i servizi da tè e da caffè, ma non li ha comprati.

Alle quattro Tony e Luisa sono andati a prendere il tè in un bar in Piazza del Duomo e Luisa gli ha fatto vedere la borsetta. Dopo due ore hanno deciso di tornare alla Rinascente perché Luisa ha visto che la cerniera della borsetta è rotta. L'ha portata indietro all'Ufficio Reclami e ha chiesto un rimborso dei soldi o un'altra borsetta. L'impiegato le ha domandato la ricevuta e dopo molte difficoltà le ha dato una borsetta nuova. Tony nel frattempo ha guardato dappertutto, ma non ha trovato niente per la madre di Luisa. Questo non è stato un pomeriggio molto fortunato per i due giovani!

Week 7

Exercise 1: 1 Perché ha mal di stomaco. 2 Sì, si preoccupa molto. 3 La deve prendere tre volte al giorno. 4 Deve tornare tra una settimana. 5 No, ha una forma leggera di gastroenterite.

Exercise 2: 1 Mi alzo alle otto. 2 Mi corico alle undici.
3 Mi lavo tutte le mattine. 4 Mi stanco a lavorare troppo.
5 Non mi arrabbio mai. 6 Mi annoio a fare la fila.
7 Mi diverto in vacanza. 8 Mi sveglio alle sette e mezzo.
9 Mi riposo dopo pranzo. 10 Mi perdo se non ho la cartina.

Exercise 3: 1 Quando cado mi faccio male. 2 Quando sono andati a letto si sono addormentati. 3 Ieri è andata dal dottore perché si è sentita male. 4 Maria è stata a letto quando si è ammalata. 5 Abbiamo fatto il bagno, poi ci siamo asciugati. 6 Non ti ho telefonato perché mi sono dimenticato/a. 7 Maria e Giovanni sono andati in chiesa e si sono sposati. 8 Non prendo più le medicine perché mi sento bene. 9 Quando sono sporchi si lavano. 10 Se scrivo la lista della spesa, mi ricordo.

Exercise 4: 1 Perché c'è stato un incidente. 2 È stato investito da un motorino. 3 Perché si è messo a correre per prendere l'autobus. 4 L'hanno portato al Pronto Soccorso. 5 Peter era alla fermata dell'autobus.

Exercise 5: 1 Sì, studiavo quando ero piccolo. 2 Sì, facevo molti sport quando ero a scuola. 3 Sì, viaggiavo molto quando abitavo in Italia. 4 Sì, andavo sempre in macchina quando lavoravo in centro. 5 Sì, sentivo molto i rumori quando dormivo al pianterreno. 6 Sì, facevamo molte gite quando eravamo in montagna. 7 Sì, andavamo fuori spesso quando abitavamo a Milano. 8 Sì, guidavamo quando avevamo diciotto anni. 9 Sì, mangiavamo solo verdura quando vivevamo in Inghilterra. 10 Sì, compravamo sempre il giornale quando lavoravamo in Italia.

Exercise 6: 1 Perché ero malato/a. 2 Perché ero indisposto/a. 3 Perché ero arrabbiato/a. 4 Perché ero troppo stanco/a. 5 Perché ero distratto/a. 6 Perché eravamo senza soldi. 7 Perché eravamo malati. 8 Perché eravamo stanchi. 9 Perché eravamo in ritardo. 10 Perché eravamo molto preoccupati.

Exercise 7: 1 Una volta viaggiavate molto. 2 Una volta ci preoccupavamo molto. 3 Una volta viaggiavano molto. 4 Una volta scrivevi molto. 5 Una volta lavorava molto. 6 Una volta mi divertivo molto. 7 Una volta uscivamo molto. 8 Una volta fumavo molto. 9 Una volta leggevi molto. 10 Una volta parlavano molto.

Exercise 8: 1 Ieri ho preso l'autobus perché ero stanca. 2 Ieri non ho guardato la televisione perché non funzionava. 3 Ieri ero a Firenze e sono andata agli Uffizi. 4 Ieri siamo andati dal dottore perché avevamo la febbre. 5 Ieri il dottore ti ha visitata a casa quando eri a letto malata. 6 Ieri sono alzata alle dieci perché era festa. 7 Ieri mentre leggevo il giornale è entrato il mio ospite. 8 Ieri mentre scrivevo la lettera i bambini hanno mangiato tutti i cioccolatini. 9 Ieri Sandra aveva mal di testa e non è andata a lavorare. 10 Ieri mentre camminavo lungo la strada ho visto un incidente.

Exercise 9: 1 Perché ha preso [si è preso] una scottatura al viso. 2 Gli prescrive una pomata. 3 Non solo sul viso ma anche sulla schiena e sulle gambe. 4 Finché l'arrossamento non è passato. 5 Se si spella deve mettere un'altra pomata protettiva.

Exercise 10:
– Ho mal di schiena.
– Da due giorni.
– Sì, mi fa molto male. È una cosa seria?
– Che cos'è uno strappo muscolare? Cosa devo fare?
– Può darmi qualcosa per il dolore?
– Grazie dottore!

Exercise 11: 1 aveva risposto 2 erano andati 3 eravate stati 4 aveva scritto 5 non aveva mai rotto 6 si era fatto male 7 era successo 8 avevo messo 9 aveva chiuso 10 ci eravamo già seduti

Week 8

Exercise 1: 1 No, secondo lei, Domingo ha una voce più calda ed espressiva. 2 Perché, secondo lui, Bocelli è il miglior tenore del mondo. 3 Tecnicamente, Bocelli canta meglio. 4 Sì, le è piaciuto. 5 No, non si interessa di sport. 6 Fa il tifo per l'Inter.

Exercise 2: 1 Ci sono più di trentamila spettatori all'Arena. 2 Secondo me, Roma è più grande di Milano. 3 Giovanni è più studioso che intelligente. 4 Ci sono più teatri a Roma che a Torino. 5 Conosco più attori italiani che stranieri. 6 Sua figlia è più alta di lei. 7 Fa più caldo in Italia che in Inghilterra. 8 Parla più piano di me. 9 Luisa mangia più di tutti. 10 L'Aida mi piace più di Rigoletto.

Exercise 3: 1 Questo è il peggior vino del mondo! 2 Siamo bravi come voi in italiano. 3 C'erano più di ventimila spettatori. 4 Maria Callas era una cantante famosissima [molto famosa]. 5 San Paolo non è grande come San Pietro. 6 Giovanni beve più caffè che acqua. 7 Mi sento meglio adesso. 8 Questi programmi sono noiosissimi [molto noiosi]. 9 Non abbiamo comprato tanti regali quanto [quanti] voi. 10 Mia sorella minore vive a Milano.

Exercise 4: 1 Vuole vedere la mostra. 2 Perché vuole andare alla Chiesa del Carmine. 3 Si trovano davanti all'Accademia. 4 Hanno comprato dei regali per i loro amici. 5 Vanno in una trattoria.

Exercise 5: 1 hanno deciso di 2 Cominciamo a 3 Spera di 4 Non mi piace 5 Ti piace 6 Preferisce 7 devono 8 Ho finito di 9 Credono [Pensano] di 10 Andiamo a

Exercise 6:
Caro Signor Rossi,
   La ringrazio del Suo invito a teatro per martedì prossimo. Mi dispiace, ma purtroppo non posso venire. Vado a Firenze martedì e non posso tornare fino a mercoledì.
   La prego di accettare le mie scuse, ma devo andare per affari e non posso rifiutare.
   Distinti saluti,

Exercise 7: 1 Io ho freddo. 2 Hanno fame. 3 Io gli do ragione! 4 ma Maria gli dà torto. 5 Tutti hanno caldo. 6 Abbiamo sete. 7 ma io gli do torto. 8 perché ho paura. 9 Hanno fretta. 10 Silvia ha torto.

Exercise 8: 1 Sì, l'abbiamo fatta. 2 Sì, ne ho fatte molte. 3 Sì, fa brutto tempo. 4 Sì, me lo fa ripetere. 5 Sì, gliela faccio vedere. 6 Sì, la facciamo in albergo. 7 Sì, me la faccio costruire. 8 Sì, ci fa fare molto lavoro. 9 Sì, ce la faccio. 10 Sì, abbiamo fatto fatica.

Exercise 9: 1 Abbiamo deciso di andare alla mostra. 2 Secondo me, questo è il peggior film di Fellini. 3 Non si sono accorti che ero stanchissimo/a. 4 Qual è il più grande teatro del mondo? 5 Non mi piace la musica tanto quanto [come] a te. 6 Gli alberghi sono più cari in agosto che in giugno. 7 Ci troviamo tra tre ore? 8 Mi dispiace molto di essere in ritardo. 9 Ti sei divertito/a con i tuoi amici ieri? 10 È riuscito/a a trovare i biglietti?

Week 9

Exercise 1: 1 Gestisce un bar. 2 È quella che parla con Tina e Mario. 3 Marco è un esperto di elettronica. 4 Lavora per una compagnia che fabbrica computer. 5 No, è Maria che fa l'avvocata.

Exercise 2: 1 che 2 cui 3 cui 4 quello che 5 Quelli che 6 che 7 quello che 8 la quale 9 cui 10 Chi

Exercise 3: 1 Dà del tu ai giovani della sua età e ai parenti. 2 Perché la conosce da quand'era bambina. 3 Alla cameriera della mensa. 4 Alle persone decisamente più vecchie di lui. 5 No, gli dà del tu.

Exercise 4: 1 Dammi quell'indirizzo. 2 Falle vedere l'ufficio. 3 Dicci la verità! 4 Valla a trovare domani. 5 Dammi del tu! 6 Stacci un po' di più! 7 Falle il biglietto. 8 Dimmi chi è! 9 Fagli una fotografia. 10 Dammi la mano!

Exercise 5: 1 No, sta salendo. 2 No, è di sinistra. 3 Perché prendono uno stipendio basso [di 1500 euro al mese]. 4 Sì, sta salendo. 5 Stanno parlando di attualità.

Exercise 6: 1 guardando 2 Studiando 3 Leggendo 4 mettendo 5 venendo 6 vendendo 7 arrivando 8 discutendo 9 Facendo 10 dicendo

Exercise 7: 1 stanno per 2 sta per 3 stanno per 4 sta per 5 stanno per 6 sta per 7 stanno per 8 stanno per 9 sta per 10 stanno per

Exercise 8:
Italy has been a republic since 1946, when there was a referendum to decide whether to keep the monarchy. The monarchy lost and the Royal Family, the House of Savoy, went into exile.

The constitution, approved in 1948, decrees that the President is Head of State but not Head of the Government: he is elected by Parliament, not by the people.

The Head of Government is the President of the Council of Ministers, with whom he/she forms the Government. This government must have the approval of both Houses.

Parliament consists of the Chamber of Deputies with 630 members and the Senate with 315. The Chamber of Deputies and the Senate are elected for five years, the President of the Republic for seven years.

Italians have the vote at the age of 18 for the parliamentary elections, but for the Senate the minimum voting age is 25. However, several political parties are in favor of reducing the voting age to 16.

Exercise 9: 1 No, è una repubblica dal 1946. 2 No, è Capo dello Stato. 3 Ci sono 630 deputati. 4 Votano a diciotto anni per la Camera e a venticinque per il Senato. 5 Ci sono 315 senatori.

Exercise 10: 1 Dammi le valigie, il treno sta per arrivare. 2 Non sapendo niente, non ho parlato. 3 Non avendo un passaporto, non posso partire. 4 Non può venire adesso perché sta mangiando. 5 Dimmi chi è! 6 Vacci subito! 7 Non scelgo mai il posto vicino al finestrino. 8 Fa così caldo oggi, sto per svenire. 9 Non posso invitarli, stanno per uscire. 10 Non conoscevo la gente con cui stava.

Week 10

Exercise 1: 1 Vanno in gita in montagna. 2 Sì, dovranno camminare per circa due ore. 3 Arriveranno verso le undici. 4 Fa l'infermiera. 5 Silvana lavora a Milano e Jeff e Tony lavorano a Londra.

Exercise 2: 1 Primo o poi verrò. 2 Prima o poi pagherò. 3 Prima o poi ballerò. 4 Prima o poi andrò. 5 Prima o poi giocherò. 6 Prima o poi sceglierò. 7 Prima o poi finirò. 8 Prima o poi ordinerò. 9 Prima o poi ritonerò. 10 Prima o poi studierò.

Exercise 3: 1 Magari verranno a piedi. 2 Magari dormiremo in tenda. 3 Magari porterete voi qualcosa da mangiare. 4 Magari usciremo più tardi. 5 Magari farà più bella figura. 6 Magari non gli daranno la mancia. 7 Magari ci aspetteranno all'altra fermata. 8 Magari canterò un'altra aria. 9 Magari pagherai tutto insieme. 10 Magari gestirà lui il ristorante.

Exercise 4: 1 Tony lavora in ospedale da tre anni, ma Jeff da due. 2 Fa quattro o cinque turni alla settimana. 3 Perché non hanno sempre gli stessi turni. 4 Sì, le piace. 5 Gli piace far collezione di francobolli.

Exercise 5: 1 di 2 da 3 di 4 da 5 di 6 alla 7 al 8 alle 9 da 10 a, dalla

Exercise 6: 1 Li ha presi in prestito da Gianni. 2 Li danno a nolo in un negozio di fianco alla posta. 3 Piove. 4 Si fermeranno al ristorante sopra alla funivia. 5 Si trovano di fronte a casa di Luisa.

Exercise 7: 1 Scriverai davvero a lui? 2 Guardo lui non lei. 3 Parla a noi, ma non a nessun altro. 4 Siete sicuri che scriverà a voi? 5 C'è molta gente prima di lui. 6 Manderai solo un regalo a lei? 7 Parlano spesso di loro. 8 Fa tutto da sé. 9 Andiamo a cavallo con loro. 10 Invitano proprio me?

Exercise 8: 1 Vi scriveremo presto. 2 Ci conosciamo da tre anni. 3 Hanno comprato una cravatta di seta per il loro padre. 4 Faccio l'infermiere/a a Firenze. 5 Hai molto da fare? 6 Voglio vedere te, non la tua ragazza! 7 Comincerò a studiare la settimana prossima. 8 Sono andati a cena da Maria. 9 Beato/a Lei! 10 L'ospedale è di fronte alla banca.

Mini-dictionary

a to, at, in
a malapena hardly
abbastanza quite, enough
abitare to live
accessori (m. pl.) accessories
accettare to accept
accomodarsi to make oneself comfortable
accordo (m.) agreement
accorgersene to notice
accorgersi to realize
acqua (f.) water
addormentarsi to fall asleep
adesso now
aereo (m.) airplane
aeroporto (m.) airport
affari (m. pl.) business
affettuoso affectionate, loving
affittare to rent, to let
affitto (m.) rental
affollato crowded
aglio (m.) garlic
agnello (m.) lamb
agosto (m.) August
aiutare to help
aiuto (m.) help
albergo (m.) hotel
alcuni/e (pl.) some, any
al di sotto below
allegro cheerful
allora then
almeno at least
alto high, tall
altrimenti otherwise
alzarsi to get up
ambulanza (f.) ambulance
ambulatorio (m.) doctor's office, clinic
ammalarsi to fall ill
ammalato ill, sick
ammobiliato furnished
analcolico nonalcoholic
anche also, too, as well, even
ancora still, again, yet

andare to go
  andare a trovare to pay a visit
animale (m.) animal
anno (m.) year
annoiarsi to get bored
antipasto (m.) hors d'œuvre
  antipasto misto variety of cured meats, olives, etc.
anziano old, elderly, senior
aperitivo (m.) aperitif
aperto open
appartamento (m.) apartment
appassionato fond, keen
approvare to approve
appuntamento (m.) appointment
appunto precisely
aprile (m.) April
aprire to open
arancia (f.) orange
arrabbiarsi to get angry
arrabbiato angry
arrivare to arrive
arrivederci goodbye
arrossamento (m.) reddening
arrosto (m.) roast
articolo (m.) article, item
artista (m. & f.) artist
artistico artistic
asciugarsi to get dry
ascoltare to listen
aspettare to wait for
aspirapolvere (m.) vacuum cleaner
assaggiare to taste
assegno (m.) check
assenza (f.) absence
attendere to wait
attento careful
attimo (m.) minute, moment
attore / attrice actor / actress
attraversare to cross
attualità (f.) current affairs
aumento (m.) increase
autobus (m.) bus

automobile (f.) car
autostrada (f.) motorway
avere to have
  aver caldo to be hot
  aver fame to be hungry
  aver freddo to be cold
  aver fretta to be in a hurry
  aver male di ... to have a
  pain in ...
  aver paura to be afraid
  aver ragione to be right
  aver sete to be thirsty
  aver torto to be wrong
  aver voglia to feel like, to want
avvisare to warn
avvocato/a lawyer

bagno (m.) bathroom
balcone (m.) balcony
bambino/a child
barba (f.) beard
basso low
basta enough
Beato/a/i/e! Lucky! (blessed)
bello beautiful
bene well
Benvenuto/a/i/e! Welcome!
benzina (f.) gasoline
bere to drink
biancheria (f.) bed linen
bianco white
bibita (f.) [soft] drink
biblioteca (f.) library
bicchiere (m.) glass
bicicletta (f.) bicycle
biglietto (m.) ticket
bistecca (f.) steak
blu blue
blusa (f.) blouse
borsa (f.) bag
Borsa (f.) Stock Exchange
borsetta (f.) handbag
braccio (m.) arm
braciola (f.) chop
bravo good, clever
brutto ugly, bad

bufalo/a buffalo
buonanotte good night
buonasera good evening
buongiorno good morning (day)
buono (m.) voucher
buono good

cadere to fall
caffè (m.) coffee
  caffè corretto coffee with a
  dash of spirits
calcio (m.) soccer
caldo hot, warm
calzature (f. pl.) footwear
cambiare to change
camera (f.) room
  camera da letto bedroom
Camera (f.) Chamber
cameriere/a waiter / waitress
camicia (f.) shirt
camminare to walk
camminata (f.) walk
campagna (f.) country
campeggio (m.) campsite
cantante (m. & f.) singer
cantare to sing
canzone (f.) song
capire to understand
capitolo (m.) chapter
capo/a head, boss
Capo/a dello Stato Head of
  State
caraffa (f.) caraffe
carne (f.) meat
caro expensive
carta (f.) map, paper
carta di credito (f.) credit card
cartina (f.) map
cartolina (f.) postcard
casa (f.) home, house
casetta (f.) small house, cottage
cassetta delle lettere (f.) mailbox
cassiere/a cashier, teller
catalogo (m.) catalog
cattivo bad
cavallo (m.) horse

cena (f.) dinner
cenare to dine
cento hundred
centro (m.) center
cercare to look for
cerniera (f.) zip, zipper
centesimo (m.) cent
certo sure, certainly
che that, what, who, whom
che cosa what
chi who?, the one/ones who
chiamare to call
chiamarsi to call oneself, to be called
chiave (f.) key
chiedere to ask
chiesa (f.) church
chilo (m.) kilo(gram)
chilometro (m.) kilometer
chiudere to close
chiuso closed
ciao hello, goodbye
cinema (m.) movies, cinema
cinquanta fifty
cinque five
cioccolatini (m. pl.) chocolates
cioccolato (m.) chocolate
ciò che what, that which
cioè that is, i.e.
circa about, approximately
città (f.) city, town
ci vuole it takes, it requires
coalizione (f.) coalition
coda (f.) queue
codice segreto (m.) PIN number
cogliere to pick
cognome (m.) family name
coincidenza (f.) coincidence
colazione (f.) breakfast
collezione (f.) collection
colore (m.) color
colpa (f.) fault
come how, like
Come mai? How come?, Why?
Come no! Certainly!, Of course!
commesso/a shop assistant

comodo comfortable
compagno/a companion, partner
compere (f. pl.) shopping, purchases
compito (m.) homework
comprare to buy
comune common
comunista (m. & f.) communist
con with
conoscere to know, to be acquainted with
consigliare to advise
consistere to consist
contento happy
conto (m.) bill
contorno (m.) side dish
contratto (m.) contract
coricarsi to lie down
correre to run
corridoio (m.) corridor
corso (m.) road, main street
cosa what?, thing
così so
costare to cost
costo (m.) cost
costruire to build
cotoletta (f.) veal cutlet
cotone (m.) cotton
cotto cooked
cravatta (f.) tie
credere to think
crema (f.) cream
criticare to criticize
cucina (f.) kitchen
cucinare to cook
cui whom, which
cuocere to cook
cupola (f.) dome
curare to cure

da from, by
  da solo alone
dappertutto everywhere
dare to give
  dare del tu/del Lei to use tu/Lei
  dare la mano to shake hands

data (f.) date
davanti a in front of
davvero really
decidere to decide
decisamente definitely
dedicarsi to devote oneself
delicato delicate, tricky
democratico democratic
dentista (m. & f.) dentist
dentro inside
deputato/a Member of
    Parliament
destra right
desiderare to wish, to want
di of
dicembre (m.) December
diciannove nineteen
di dove? where from?
dieci ten
dieta (f.) diet
dietro a behind
differenza (f.) difference
difficile difficult
difficoltà (f.) difficulty
di fronte a opposite
digitare to key in
dimenticarsi to forget
dipendere to depend
di più more
di preciso exactly
dire to say
direttore / direttrice
    director, manager
diritto straight
disastro (m.) disaster
discutere to discuss
di solito usually
dispiacersi to be sorry
distanza (f.) distance
distinto distinguished
distratto absent-minded, distracted
disturbare to bother
disturbo (m.) bother, disturbance
dito (m.) finger, toe
ditta (f.) firm, company
di turno on duty

diventare to become
diversi (pl.) several
diverso different
divertirsi to enjoy oneself
divisa (f.) uniform
doccia (f.) shower
documento (m.) document
dodici twelve
dolore (m.) pain
domandare to ask
domani tomorrow
domenica (f.) Sunday
dopo after, later, then
doppio double
dormire to sleep
dottore / dottoressa doctor
dove where
dovere to have to, must
droghiere (m.) grocer's
due two
dunque so, then
duomo (m.) cathedral
durare to last, to endure
durata (f.) duration
duro hard

e and
eccetto except
ecco here's, here it is
eleggere to elect
elettronica (f.) electronics
elezioni (f. pl.) elections
ente (m.) body, organization, board
entrare in vigore to become law
esaminare to examine
esilio (m.) exile
esperto/a expert
esporsi al sole to be exposed to the
    sun, to sunbathe
espressivo intense, with feeling
essere to be
    essere abituato a to be used to
    essere nato to be born
est (m.) east
estate (f.) summer
età (f.) age

etto (m.) 100 grams
euro (m. sing.) euro
evitare to avoid
extra extra

fabbricare to manufacture
facchino (m.) porter
facile easy
facilmente easily
fame (f.) hunger
famiglia (f.) family
famoso famous
fantastico great
far bella figura to look good, to
  impress
farcela to manage, to cope
far conoscenza to get acquainted
fare to do, to make
farmacia (f.) pharmacy
farmacista (m. & f.) pharmacist
far male to hurt
far vedere to show
fatica (f.) effort
febbraio (m.) February
febbre (f.) temperature, fever
fermarsi to stop, to stay
fermata (f.) stop
ferroviere/a railroad worker
festa (f.) feast (day), party
figlia (f.) daughter
figlio (m.) son, child
figura (f.) figure
figurati sure, no problem (fam.)
finalmente at last
finché ... non until
finestra (f.) window
finire to finish
fino a as far as
finocchio (m.) fennel
Firenze (f.) Florence
fissare to arrange
foglio (m.) sheet of paper
forma (f.) form, shape
formare to form
forno (m.) oven
forse perhaps

fortunato lucky
francobollo (m.) stamp
fratello (m.) brother
freddo cold
fresco fresh, cool
fretta (f.) hurry
frizzante fizzy
frutta (f.) fruit
fruttivendolo (m.) produce market
fumare to smoke
funivia (f.) cable car
funzionare to work, to function
fuori outside

gabinetto (m.) lavatory, toilet
galleria (f.) gallery
gamba (f.) leg
garage (m.) garage
gastroenterite (f.) gastroenteritis
gelato (m.) ice cream
gelato frozen
generale general
genio (m.) genius
genitori (m. pl.) parents
gennaio (m.) January
Genova (f.) Genoa
gente (f. sing.) people
gentile kind
gestire to run (a business)
già already
giardino (m.) garden
ginocchio (m.) knee
giocare to play (a game)
giornalaio (m.) newsdealer's
giornale (m.) newspaper
giornalista (m. & f.) journalist
giorno (m.) day
giovane young
giovedì (m.) Thursday
gita (f.) trip, excursion
giugno (m.) June
giusto correct
gnocchi (m. pl.) potato dumplings
governo (m.) government
grado (m.) degree
grande big

grata (f.) shutter
gratis free (of charge)
grazie thank you
griglia (f.) grill
grissino (m.) breadstick
guardare to see
guida (m. & f.) guide
guidare to drive

hobby (m.) hobby

idea (f.) idea
ieri yesterday
ignorare to ignore
il (m.) the
il quale who, whom,
   which, that
imbucare to post
imparare to learn
impegnato busy, engaged
impiegato/a clerk, employee
importante important
impostare to set up, to plan
incidente (m.) accident
in cima a on top of
incontrarsi to meet
indietro back, behind
indirizzo (m.) address
indisposto indisposed, unwell
infermiere/a nurse
inflazione (f.) inflation
in fondo a at the end of
informazione (f.) information
Inghilterra (f.) England
inglese (m. & f.) English
in orario on time
in pensione retired
inquilino/a tenant
in ritardo late, delayed
insalata (f.) salad
insegnante (m. & f.) teacher
insieme a together with
insistere to insist
insuperabile unequaled,
   outstanding
intelligente intelligent, clever

intendere to understand
interessarsi to be interested
interno (m.) interior
interrompere to interrupt
in tutto altogether
invece instead
inverno (m.) winter
investire to run over, to hit
invitare to invite
invito (m.) invitation
istituto (m.) institute, faculty
Italia (f.) Italy
italiano/a Italian

la (f.) the
labbro (m.) lip
lana (f.) wool
lasagne (f. pl.) lasagne
lasciare to let, to leave
laterale on the side
lavanderia (f.) laundry area,
   launderette
lavapiatti (f.) dishwasher
lavarsi to wash oneself
lavatrice (f.) washing machine
lavorare to work
lavoro (m.) work
leggero light, mild
legno (m.) wood
lei she
Lei you (formal)
lettera (f.) letter
lettino (m.) examination table
letto (m.) bed
lezione (f.) lesson
li there
liberale liberal
libero free (available)
lingua (f.) language
lirica (f.) operatic music
lista (f.) list
Londra (f.) London
lontano da far from
luce light
luglio (m.) July
lunedì (m.) Monday

ma but
madre (f.) mother
magari perhaps
maglione (m.) sweater
maiale (m.) pig, pork
macchina (f.) car, machine
maggio (m.) May
maggiore greater, greatest, older, oldest
magnifico magnificent
malattia (f.) illness, disease
male badly
mancia (f.) tip
mandare to send
mangiare to eat
mano (f.) hand
mantenere to keep
manzo (m.) beef
mare (m.) sea
marito (m.) husband
martedì (m.) Tuesday
marzo (m.) March
matita (f.) pencil
mattino (m.) morning
media (f.) average
medicina (f.) medicine
medico/a (medical) doctor
meglio better (adv.)
membro (m. & f.) member
meno less, least
Meno male! Thank goodness!
mensa (f.) refectory, canteen
mercato (m.) market
mercoledì (m.) Wednesday
mese (m.) month
metropolitana (f.) metro
mettere to put
mezzanotte (f.) midnight
mezzo half, means
mezzogiorno (m.) midday
Mi dispiace I'm sorry
migliore better, best
Milano (f.) Milan
milione (m.) million
mille thousand
　mille grazie many thanks

minerale mineral
minestra (f.) soup
minimo minimum
minore smaller/-est, younger/-est
minuto (m.) minute
mio my, mine
mi pare I think, it seems to me
mi piace I like
Mi raccomando! Be sure to ...!
misura (f.) size
mobili (m. pl.) furniture
moderno modern
moglie (f.) wife
molto very, much
molto lieto pleased (to meet you)
momento (m.) moment
monarchia (f.) monarchy
mondo (m.) world
montagna (f.) mountain
monte (m.) mount, mountain
morire to die
morto dead
mosso rough (sea)
mostra (f.) exhibition
motocicletta (f.) motorcycle
motorino (m.) scooter
mucca (f.) cow
muscolare muscular
musica (f.) music

Napoli (f.) Naples
nato/a born
nazionale national
neanche neither, not even
necessario necessary
negozio (m.) shop
nel frattempo in the meantime
nessuno/a no one
niente nothing
no no
noioso boring
noleggiare to rent, to hire
noleggio, nolo (m.) rental, hire
non not
non veder l'ora di to look forward to

nome (m.) name
nord (m.) north
notizie (f. pl.) news
notte (f.) night
novanta ninety
nove nine
novembre (m.) November
numero (m.) number
nuotare to swim
nuovo new

obbligatorio compulsory
occasione (f.) opportunity
occhiali (m. pl.) eyeglasses
occhiata (f.) look, glance
occupato busy
occupazione (f.) occupation
offrire to offer
oggi today
ogni every
olio (m.) oil
oliva (f.) olive
opera (f.) opera
ora (f.) hour, time (of the day)
orario (m.) timetable
ordinare to order, to put in order
orecchio (m.) ear
orologiaio/a watchmaker
ospedale (m.) hospital
ospite (m. & f.) guest
osteria (f.) bar, tavern, pub
ottanta eighty
otto eight
ottobre (m.) October
ovest (m.) west

padre (m.) father
padrone/a [di casa] landlord,
   landlady
pane (m.) bread
panino (m.) bread roll, sandwich
pantofole (f. pl.) slippers
Papa (m.) Pope
parente (m. & f.) relative
parlamentare parliamentary
Parlamento (m.) Parliament

parlare to speak
parmigiano (m.) Parmesan
partire to leave
partita (f.) match
partito (m.) (political) party
passaporto (m.) passport
passare to pass
passatempo (m.) pastime
passeggero/a passenger
passeggiata (f.) walk
passione (f.) passion, interest
pastina (f.) pastry
pasto (m.) meal
patata (f.) potato
patate fritte (f. pl.) fries
paura (f.) fear
Pavia (f.) Pavia
paziente patient
pazzo mad, crazy, insane
peggio worse (adv.)
peggiore worse/worst
pelle (f.) leather
pensare to think
pensionante (m. & f.) paying
   guest
pensionato/a retired
pensione completa (f.) full board
per for
per cento percent
perché why, because
perdere to lose
perdersi to get lost
per esempio for example
per favore / per piacere please
periferia (f.) suburbs
permettere to allow
personale personal
per terra on the floor/ground
pesce (m.) fish
pessimo very bad
pezzo (m.) piece
piacere nice to meet you, pleasure
piacevole pleasant
piangere to weep, to cry
pianista (m & f.) pianist
piano (m.) floor, story

piano slowly
piano, pianoforte (m.) piano
pianterreno (m.) ground floor
piantina (f.) map
piatto (m.) dish
piazza (f.) public square
piccolo small
piedi (m. pl.) feet
pieno full
piscina (f.) swimming pool
poco little
poi then
Policlinico (m.) General Hospital
Politecnico (m.) polytechnic
politica (f.) politics
pomata (f.) cream, ointment
pomeriggio (m.) afternoon
pomodoro (m.) tomato
popolo (m.) people
porta (f.) door
portare to carry, to bring, to wear
portare di ritorno/indietro
  to bring back
portavoce (m. & f.) spokesperson
portinaio/a doorkeeper, concierge
possibile possible
posta (f.) mail, post, post office
posto (m.) seat, place
potere to be able to
povero poor
pranzo (m.) lunch
preciso precise
preferire to prefer
preferito favorite
pregare to pray, to beg
prego you're welcome, please
premere to press
prendere to take
  prendere in prestito to borrow
prenotare to book, to reserve
preoccuparsi to be worried
preparare to prepare
prescrivere to prescribe
presentare to introduce
presidente (m. & f.) president,
  chairperson

Presidente del Consiglio
  (m. & f.) prime minister
prestare to lend
prestito (m.) loan
presto early
presuntuoso conceited
Pretura (f.) Police Headquarters
prezzo (m.) price
prima colazione (f.) breakfast
prima di before
primo first
  primo piatto (m.) first course
probabilmente probably
programma (m.) program
pronto soccorso (m.) ER
proprietario/a owner
proprio really, quite
prossimo next
protettivo protective
pulire to clean
purtroppo unfortunately

quanto how, how much
qualche some
qualcosa something
qual(e) what, which
qualsiasi whatever, any
qualunque whatever, any
quando when
quaranta forty
quarto fourth
quattordici fourteen
quattro four
questione (f.) matter, issue,
  question
questo this
qui here
quindici fifteen
quotidiano daily

radersi to shave
radio (f.) radio
ragazzo/a boy, boyfriend
  girl, girlfriend (age ~15–25)
ragione (f.) right, reason
recitare to act

reclami (m. pl.) complaints
referendum (m.) referendum
regalare to give (as a present)
regalo (m.) present, gift
regata (f.) regatta
regionale regional
regione (f.) region
regnante ruling
reparto (m.) department
repubblica (f.) republic
repubblicano republican
restare to stay, to remain
restaurare to restore
ricetta (f.) prescription
ricevere to receive
ricevuta (f.) receipt
riconoscere to recognize
ricordarsi to remember
ricotta (f.) ricotta cheese
riduzione (f.) reduction, decrease
rifiutare to refuse
riga (f.) stripe, line
rilassarsi to relax
rimanere to stay
rimborso (m.) refund
rimodernare to modernize
riparare to mend
riposarsi to rest
riservare to book, to reserve
risparmiare to save
rispondere to reply
ristorante (m.) restaurant
ritardo (m.) delay
riuscire to succeed
rivedere to see again
rivista (f.) magazine
roba (f.) belongings, things
rompere to break
rosso red
roulotte (f.) caravan
rumore (m.) noise
russo/a Russian
rustico (m.) farmhouse

sabato (m.) Saturday
salotto (m.) lounge, living room

sala da pranzo (m.) dining room
salame (m.) salami
salire to climb, to go up
salutare to greet
salute (f.) health, Cheers!
sapere to know (how)
sbagliato wrong
scarpe (f. pl.) shoes
scarponi (m. pl.) boots
scatola (f.) box
scegliere to choose
scendere to go down, to descend
scelta (f.) choice
schermo (m.) screen
schiena (f.) back (part of body)
sci (m. pl.) skis
sciare to ski
sciogliere to dissolve
sciopero (m.) strike (labor)
scompartimento (m.)
   compartment
scottatura (f.) burn
scrivania (f.) desk
scrivere to write
scuola (f.) school
   scuola elementare
   elementary school
   scuola media middle school
scusa (f.) excuse
scusare to excuse, to forgive
se if, whether
secco dry
secolo (m.) century
secondo according to, in the
   opinion of
secondo second
sedersi to sit down
sedici sixteen
segretario/a secretary
segreto secret
seguire to follow
sei six
semaforo (m.) traffic light
sempre always
Senato (m.) Senate
senatore / senatrice senator

senso (m.) way, sense
sentire to hear
sentirsi to feel
serio serious
servire to serve
servizi (m. pl.) facilities
servizio (m.) set, service
sessanta sixty
sesto sixth
seta (f.) silk
sete (f.) thirst
settanta seventy
sette seven
settembre (m.) September
settimana (f.) week
sgabuzzino (m.) closet
sgonfio flat (tire)
si one, oneself, him/herself, themselves
sì yes
sicuro sure
signora (f.) Mrs., madam, Ms.
signore (m.) Mr., sir
signorina (f.) Miss, young lady
simpatico likable
sincero sincere
sindacato (m.) trade union
singolo single
sinistra left
sistema (m.) system
socialista (m. & f.) socialist
società (f.) company
soggiorno (m.) stay, living room
soldi (m. pl.) money
sole (m.) sun
solo only
soprattutto mainly
sorella (f.) sister
sotto below, under
spaghetti (m. pl.) spaghetti
Spagna (f.) Spain
spazioso roomy
specialità (f.) specialty
specialmente specially
spellarsi to peel
spendere to spend

spesa (f.) shopping
spesso often
spettacolo (m.) show, spectacle
spettatore / spettatrice spectator
spiegare to explain
sporcarsi to get dirty
sporco dirty
sportello (m.) (train) door
sposarsi to get married
stabilire to establish, to decide on
stadio (m.) stadium
stamattina this morning
stancarsi to get tired
stanco tired
stanza (f.) room
stazione (f.) station
stesso the same
stomaco (m.) stomach
storia (f.) story, history
storico historical
strada (f.) road
straniero/a foreign, foreigner
strappo (m.) sprain
studente / studentessa student
studiare to study
studioso studious
stupido stupid
su on
subito immediately
succedere to happen
sud (m.) south
suo his/hers, yours (form.)
suocero/a father/mother-in-law
suonare to play (an instrument), to ring
supermercato (m.) supermarket
svago (m.) pastime
svegliarsi to wake up
svendita (f.) sale
svestirsi to undress

tabaccaio (m.) tobacconist
tanto ... quanto as ... as
tardi late
tartina (f.) canapé, hors d'œuvre
tassa di soggiorno (f.) tourist tax

taxi (m.) taxi
teatro (m.) theater
telefonare to phone
telefono (m.) telephone
telegramma (m.) telegram
televisione (f.) television
tempo (m.) time (general)
tenda (f.) tent
tenere to keep, to hold
tenore (m.) tenor
terrazzo (m.) terrace
tesi (f.) thesis
testa (f.) head
tifo (m.) support, cheer
   fare il tifo per to support,
   to cheer
tifoso/a fan, supporter
tinello (m.) small dining room
tocca a me it's my turn
tornare to go/come back, to return
torto (m.) wrong
tra among, between
tragico tragic
trasporto (m.) transportation
tre three
tredici thirteen
treno (m.) train
trenta thirty
troppo too, too much
trota (f.) trout
trovare to find
trovarsi to meet
turno (m.) duty, shift
tuttavia however

un, una a, an
undici eleven
ufficio (m.) office
   ufficio postale (m.) post office
uguale same, equal
unico unique
università (f.) university
uno one
un po' a little
usare to use
uscire to go out

vacanza (f.) vacation, holiday
vagone (m.) carriage
valigia (f.) suitcase
vecchio old
vedere to see
vegetariano/a vegetarian
vendita (f.) sale
venerdì (m.) Friday
Venezia (f.) Venice
venire to come
venti twenty
veramente really
verde green
verdura (f.) vegetable
verità (f.) truth
vero true
vestirsi to get dressed
vestito (m.) dress, suit
vettura (f.) carriage
viaggiare to travel
vicino near
violinista (m. & f.) violinist
visita (f.) visit
visitare to visit, to examine
viso (m.) face
vita (f.) life
vitello (m.) veal
voce (f.) voice
voglia (f.) wish
volentieri willingly, gladly
volere to want, to wish
volo (m.) flight
volta (f.) time (occasion)
votare to vote
voto (m.) vote
vuoto empty

weekend (m.) weekend

zanzara (f.) mosquito
zero (m.) zero, nought
zio / zia (f.) uncle / aunt
zoo (m.) zoo
zucchero (m.) sugar

a, an un, una, uno
a little un po'
absence assenza (f.)
(to) accept accettare
accessories accessori (m. pl.)
accident incidente (m.)
according to secondo
(to) act recitare
actor / actress attore / attrice
address indirizzo (m.)
advice consiglio (m.)
(to) advise consigliare
affectionate affettuoso
after dopo, poi
afternoon pomeriggio (m.)
again ancora
age età (f.)
agreement accordo (m.)
airplane aeroplano, aereo (m.)
airport aeroporto (m.)
(to) allow permettere
alone da solo
already già
also anche
altogether in tutto
always sempre
ambulance ambulanza (f.)
among fra, tra
and e
angry arrabbiato
animal animale (m.)
any alcuni, qualsiasi, qualunque
aperitif aperitivo (m.)
appointment appuntamento (m.)
(to) approve approvare
approximately circa
April aprile (m.)
arm braccio (m.)
(to) arrange fissare
(to) arrive arrivare
article (item) articolo (m.)
artist artista (m. & f.)
artistic artistico
as ... as tanto ... quanto
as far as fino a

(to) ask chiedere, domandare
as well anche
at a, in
at last finalmente
at least almeno
at the end of in fondo a
aunt zia (f.)
August agosto (m.)
average media (f.)
(to) avoid evitare

back (part of body) schiena (f.)
bad cattivo, brutto
badly male
bag borsa (f.)
balcony balcone (m.)
bank banca (f.)
bar osteria (f.)
bathroom bagno (m.)
(to) be essere
(to) be afraid avere paura
(to) be born essere nato/a
(to) be called chiamarsi
(to) be cold avere freddo
(to) be hot avere caldo
(to) be hungry avere fame
(to) be in a hurry avere fretta
(to) be right avere ragione
(to) be thirsty avere sete
(to) be used to essere abituato a
(to) be wrong avere torto
Be sure to ... Mi raccomando ...
beard barba (f.)
beautiful bello
because perché
because of a causa di
(to) become diventare
(to) become law entrare in vigore
bed letto (m.)
bed linen biancheria (f.)
bedroom camera da letto (m.)
beef manzo (m.)
before prima di
(to) beg pregare
(to) begin cominciare

behind dietro a
(to) believe credere
belongings roba (f.)
below sotto
beside a fianco di
better (adv.) meglio
better, best migliore
between fra, tra
bicycle bicicletta (f.)
big grande
bill conto (m.)
blouse blusa (f.)
blue blu
boarding school collegio (m.)
body (institution) ente (m.)
(to) book prenotare, riservare
boots scarponi (m. pl.)
boring noioso
born nato/a
(to) borrow prendere in prestito
boss capo/a
(to) bother disturbare
box scatola (f.)
boy ragazzo (m.)
boyfriend ragazzo (m.)
bread pane (m.)
bread roll panino (m.)
(to) break rompere
breakfast colazione (f.)
brother fratello (m.)
buffalo bufalo/a
(to) build costruire
burn scottatura (f.)
bus autobus (m.)
business affari (m. pl.)
busy occupato, impegnato
but ma
(to) buy comprare
by da
bye arrivederci

cable car funivia, funicolare (f.)
cake (pastry) pastina (f.)
(to) call chiamare
    (to be) called chiamarsi
campsite campeggio (m.)

can (vb.) potere
canapé tartina (f.)
canteen mensa (f.)
car automobile, macchina (f.)
carafe caraffa (f.)
caravan roulotte (f.)
careful attento
    (to be) careful stare attento
carriage vagone (m.), vettura (f.)
(to) carry portare
cashier cassiere/a
catalog catalogo (m.)
cathedral duomo (m.)
cent centesimo (m.)
center centro (m.)
century secolo (m.)
certainly certo
Certainly! Of course! Come no!
Chamber Camera (f.)
(to) change cambiare
chapter capitolo (m.)
check assegno (m.)
cheerful allegro
Cheers! Salute!
child bambino/a
chocolate cioccolato (m.)
chocolates cioccolatini (m. pl.)
choice scelta (f.)
(to) choose scegliere
chop braciola (f.)
church chiesa (f.)
cinema cinema (m.)
city città (f.)
(to) clean pulire
clever bravo
(to) climb salire
(to) close chiudere
closed chiuso
closet sgabuzzino (m.)
coalition coalizione (f.)
coffee caffè (m.)
coincidence coincidenza (f.)
cold freddo (m.)
collection collezione (f.)
color colore (m.)
(to) come venire

comfortable comodo
companion compagno/a
company società (f.)
compartment scompartimento (m.)
complaint reclamo (m.)
compulsory obbligatorio
conceited presuntuoso
(to) consist consistere
contract contratto (m.)
(to) cook cucinare, cuocere
cooked cotto
(to) cope farcela
correct giusto
corridor corridoio (m.)
cost costo (m.)
(to) cost costare
cottage casetta (f.)
cotton cotone (m.)
couch lettino (m.)
countryside campagna (f.)
course (dish) piatto (m.)
cow mucca (f.)
cream crema (f.)
credit card carta di credito (f.)
critical care pronto soccorso (m.)
(to) criticize criticare
(to) cross attraversare
crowded affollato
(to) cure curare
current affairs attualità (f.)

dad, daddy papà, babbo (m.)
daily quotidiano
date data (f.)
daughter figlia (f.)
day giorno (m.)
dead morto
December dicembre (m.)
(to) decide decidere
definitely decisamente
degree grado (m.)
delicate delicato
democratic democratico
dentist dentista (m. & f.)
department reparto (m.)
(to) depend dipendere

desk scrivania (f.)
(to) determine stabilire
(to) devote oneself dedicarsi
(to) die morire
diet dieta (f.)
difference differenza (f.)
different diverso
difficult difficile
difficulty difficoltà (f.)
(to) dine cenare
dining room sala da pranzo (f.),
   (small) tinello (m.)
dinner cena (f.)
director direttore, direttrice
dirty sporco
   (to get) dirty sporcarsi
(to) discuss discutere
disease malattia (m.)
dish piatto (m.)
dishwasher lavapiatti (f.)
(to) dissolve sciogliere
distance distanza (f.)
distracted distratto
(to) do fare
doctor medico/a, dottore/ssa
document documento (m.)
dome cupola (f.)
door porta (f.)
doorbell campanello (m.)
doorkeeper portinaio/a
double doppio
dress vestito (m.)
(to get) dressed vestirsi
drink (soft) bibita (f.)
(to) drink bere
(to) drive guidare
dry secco
(to) dry oneself asciugarsi
dumplings gnocchi (m. pl.)
duration durata
duty turno (m.)
   on duty di turno

ear orecchio (m.)
early presto
easily facilmente

east est (m.)
easy facile
(to) eat mangiare
effort fatica
eight otto
eighteen diciotto
eighty ottanta
(to) elect eleggere
elections elezioni (f. pl.)
electronics elettronica (f.)
elementary school scuola
    elementare (f.)
eleven undici
empty vuoto
England Inghilterra (f.)
English inglese (m. & f.)
(to) enjoy oneself divertirsi
enough abbastanza
equal uguale
(to) establish stabilire
eventually alla fine
every ogni
everywhere dappertutto
exactly di preciso
examination esame (m.)
(to) examine esaminare
except eccetto
excuse scusa (f.)
(to) excuse scusare
exhibition mostra (f.)
exile esilio (m.)
expensive caro
expert esperto/a
(to) explain spiegare

face viso (m.), faccia (f.)
facilities servizi (m. pl.)
(to) fall cadere
(to) fall ill ammalarsi
family famiglia (f.)
famous famoso
fantastic fantastico
far from lontano da
farmhouse fattoria (f.),
    rustico (m.)
fast veloce

father padre (m.)
fault colpa (f.)
favorite preferito
fear paura (f.)
feast festa (f.)
February febbraio (m.)
(to) feel sentirsi
(to) feel like (want to)
    aver voglia (di)
feet piedi (m. pl.)
fennel finocchio (m.)
fever febbre (f.)
few alcuni, pochi (pl.)
fifteen quindici
fifty cinquanta
figure figura (f.)
(to) find trovare
finger dito (m.)
(to) finish finire
firm (company) ditta (f.)
first primo
fish pesce (m.)
five cinque
fizzy frizzante
flat appartamento (m.)
flat (tyre) sgonfio
flight volo (m.)
floor (storey) piano (m.)
Florence Firenze (f.)
(to) follow seguire
fond appassionato
footwear calzature (f. pl.)
for per
foreign, foreigner straniero/a
for example per esempio
(to) forget dimenticarsi
form forma (f.)
(to) form formare
forty quaranta
four quattro
fourteen quattordici
fourth quarto
free (available) libero
fresh fresco
Friday venerdì (m.)
friend amico/a

from da
frozen gelato
fruit frutta (f.)
full pieno
(to) function funzionare
furnished ammobiliato
furniture mobili (m. pl.)

gallery galleria (f.)
garage garage (m.)
garden giardino (m.)
garlic aglio (m.)
gasoline benzina (f.)
gastroenteritis gastroenterite (f.)
general generale
General Hospital Policlinico (m.)
genius genio (m.)
(to) get (become) diventare
(to) get (obtain) ottenere
(to) get angry arrabbiarsi
(to) get bored annoiarsi
(to) get dirty sporcarsi
(to) get dressed vestirsi
(to) get dry asciugarsi
(to) get lost perdersi
(to) get married sposarsi
(to) get tired stancarsi
(to) get undressed svestirsi
(to) get up alzarsi
(to) get worried preoccuparsi
girl ragazza (f.)
girlfriend ragazza (f.)
(to) give dare
(to) give (as a present) regalare
glass bicchiere (m.)
glasses (eye) occhiali (m. pl.)
(to) go andare
(to) go down scendere
(to) go out uscire
(to) go up salire
good buono, bravo
goodbye ciao, arrivederci
good evening buonasera
good morning/day buongiorno
good night buonanotte
greater, greatest maggiore

green verde
(to) greet salutare
grill griglia (f.)
grocer's droghiere (m.)
ground floor pianterreno (m.)
guest ospite (m. & f.)
guesthouse pensione (f.)
guide guida (m. & f.)

half mezzo
ham prosciutto (m.)
hand mano (f.)
handbag borsetta (f.)
(to) happen succedere
happy contento
hard duro
hardly appena, a malapena
(to) have avere
(to) have a pain in ... aver male
 di ...
head testa (f.)
Head of State Capo/a dello Stato
(to) hear sentire
hello ciao
help aiuto (m.)
(to) help aiutare
here qui
here it is, here's ecco
high alto
historical storico
hobby hobby, passatempo (m.)
holiday vacanza (f.)
homework compito (m.)
hors d'œuvre antipasto (m.)
horse cavallo (m.)
hospital ospedale (m.)
hostel ostello (m.)
hot caldo
hotel albergo (m.)
hour ora (f.)
house casa (f.)
how come
How come?, Why? Come mai?
how, how much quanto
however tuttavia
hundred cento

hunger fame (m.)
hurry fretta (f.)
(to) hurry up affrettarsi
(to) hurt far male
husband marito (m.)

ice cream gelato (m.)
idea idea (f.)
if se
(to) ignore ignorare
ill ammalato, malato
illness malattia (m.)
immediately subito
important importante
in in
increase aumento (m.)
inflation inflazione (f.)
information informazione (f.)
in front of davanti a
inside interno (m.), dentro
instead invece
institute istituto (m.)
(to) introduce presentare
intelligent intelligente
intense (in feeling) espressivo
(to be) interested interessarsi
(to) interrupt interrompere
invitation invito (m.)
(to) invite invitare
Italian italiano
Italy Italia (f.)

January gennaio (m.)
journalist giornalista
  (m. & f.)
July luglio (m.)
June giugno (m.)

(to) keep tenere,
  mantenere
key chiave (f.)
(to) key in digitare
kilo(gram) chilo (m.)
kilometer chilometro (m.)
kind gentile
kitchen cucina (f.)

knee ginocchio (m.)
(to) know conoscere
(to) know (how) sapere

lady signora (f.)
lake lago (m.)
lamb agnello (m.)
landlord/lady padrone/a
language lingua (f.)
lasagne lasagne (f. pl.)
late in ritardo, tardi
laundry area, laundrette
  lavanderia (f.)
lawyer avvocato/a
(to) learn imparare
leather pelle (f.)
(to) leave partire
(to) leave (let) lasciare
left sinistra
leg gamba (f.)
(to) lend prestare
less, least meno
lesson lezione (f.)
(to) let (leave) lasciare
(to) let (rent) affittare
letter lettera (f.)
liberal liberale
library biblioteca (f.)
(to) lie down coricarsi
life vita (f.)
light luce (f.)
light leggero
like come
(to) like piacere
likable simpatico
line riga (f.)
lip labbro (m.)
list lista (f.)
(to) listen ascoltare
(a) little un po'
(to) live abitare
loan prestito (m.)
London Londra (f.)
look (glance) occhiata (f.)
(to) look at guardare
(to) look for cercare

(to) look forward to non veder
l'ora di
(to) lose perdere
lounge (living room) salotto (m.)
low basso
lucky fortunato, beato
lunch pranzo (m.)

mad (crazy) pazzo
madam signora (f.)
magazine rivista (f.)
magnificent magnifico
mail posta (f.)
mailbox cassetta delle
lettere (f.)
mainly soprattutto
(to) make fare
(to) manage farcela
manager direttore/direttrice
(to) manufacture fabbricare
map cartina, carta, piantina (f.)
March marzo (m.)
market mercato (m.)
marvelous stupendo,
meraviglioso
match (game) partita (f.)
matter questione (f.)
May maggio (m.)
maybe forse
meal pasto (m.)
means mezzo (m.)
meanwhile nel frattempo
meat carne (f.)
medicine medicina (f.)
(to) meet incontrarsi, trovarsi
member membro (m. & f.)
Member of Parliament
deputato/a
(to) mend riparare
metro metropolitana (f.)
midday mezzogiorno (m.)
middle school scuola media (f.)
midnight mezzanotte (f.)
Milan Milano (f.)
million milione (m.)
mine mio

mineral minerale
minimum minimo
minute minuto (m.)
Miss signorina (f.)
mom, mommy mamma (f.)
modern moderno
(to) modernize rimodernare
moment momento (m.),
attimo (m.)
monarchy monarchia (f.)
Monday lunedì (m.)
money soldi (m. pl.)
month mese (m.)
more più, di più
morning mattino (m.)
   this morning stamattina
mosquito zanzara (f.)
mother madre (f.)
mother-in-law suocera (f.)
motorcycle motocicletta (f.)
motorway autostrada (f.)
mount monte (m.)
mountain montagna (f.)
Mr. signore (m.)
Mrs., Ms. signora (f.)
much molto
muscular muscolare
must (vb.) dovere
my mio

name nome (m.)
   family name cognome (m.)
national nazionale
near vicino
necessary necessario
new nuovo
news notizie (f. pl.)
newsdealer's giornalaio (m.)
newspaper giornale (m.)
next prossimo
next to accanto a, a fianco di
night notte (f.)
nine nove
ninety novanta
no no
noise rumore (m.)

nonalcoholic analcolico
no one nessuno/a
north nord (m.)
not non
nothing niente, nulla
(to) notice accorgersene
nought zero (m.)
November novembre
now adesso
number numero (m.)
nurse infermiere/a

occupation occupazione (f.)
of di
(to) offer offrire
office ufficio (m.)
often spesso
oil olio (m.)
ointment pomata (f.)
old vecchio, anziano
olive oliva (f.)
on su
on the side laterale
on top of in cima a
one uno
(the) one/ones who chi
only solo
open aperto
(to) open aprire
operatic music lirica (f.)
opportunity occasione (f.)
opposite di fronte a
orange arancia (f.)
(to) order ordinare
otherwise altrimenti
outside fuori
oven forno (m.)
owner proprietario/a

pain dolore (m.)
parents genitori (m. pl.)
Parliament parlamento (m.)
parliamentary parlamentare
Parmesan parmigiano (m.)
partner compagno/a
party partito (m.)

(to) pass passare
passenger passeggero/a
passion passione (f.)
passport passaporto (m.)
pastime svago (m.)
pastry pastina (f.)
patient paziente
(to) pay pagare
(to) pay attention stare attento
paying guest pensionante (m. & f.)
(to) peel spellarsi
pencil matita (f.)
people popolo (m.), gente (f.)
percent per cento
perhaps forse, magari
personal personale
pharmacist farmacista (m. & f.)
pharmacy farmacia (f.)
(to) phone telefonare
pianist pianista (m. & f.)
piano piano, pianoforte (m.)
(to) pick cogliere
piece pezzo (m.)
pig maiale (m.)
PIN number codice segreto (m.)
place posto (m.)
(to) play (a game) giocare
(to) play (an instrument) suonare
pleasant piacevole, simpatico
please per favore, per piacere,
  prego
pleased to meet you molto lieto,
  piacere
politics politica (f.)
polytechnic Politecnico (m.)
poor povero
Pope Papa (m.)
porter facchino (m.)
possible possibile
(to) post imbucare
post office posta (f.), ufficio
  postale (m.)
potato patata (f.)
(to) pray pregare
precisely appunto
(to) prefer preferire

(to) prepare preparare
(to) prescribe prescrivere
prescription ricetta (f.)
present regalo (m.)
president presidente (m. & f.)
(to) press premere
price prezzo (m.)
prime minister presidente del
    consiglio (m. & f.)
probably probabilmente
produce market fruttivendolo (m.)
program programma (m.)
protective protettivo
purchase compera (f.)
(to) put mettere

question questione (f.)
queue coda (f.)
quite abbastanza

radio radio (f.)
railroad worker ferroviere/a
(to) rain piovere
(to) realize accorgersi
really proprio, veramente
reason ragione (f.)
receipt ricevuta (f.)
(to) receive ricevere
(to) recognize riconoscere
red rosso
reddening arrossamento (m.)
reduction riduzione (f.)
refectory mensa (f.)
referendum referendum (m.)
regatta regata (f.)
region regione (f.)
regional regionale
relative parente (m. & f.)
(to) remain restare
(to) remember ricordarsi
(to) rent affittare
rental affitto (m.)
rental, hire noleggio, nolo (m.)
(to) reply rispondere
republic repubblica (f.)
republican repubblicano

(to) rest riposarsi
restaurant ristorante (m.)
(to) restore restaurare
retired in pensione, pensionato/a
right destra
right (reason) ragione (f.)
(to) ring suonare
road strada (f.), via (f.), corso (m.)
roast arrosto (m.)
Rome Roma (f.)
room camera (f.), stanza (f.)
roomy spazioso
rough (sea) mosso
ruling regnante
(to) run correre
(to) run a business gestire
(to) run over investire
Russian russo/a

salad insalata (f.)
salami salame (m.)
sale vendita (f.)
sales svendita (f.)
same stesso, uguale
Saturday sabato (m.)
(to) save risparmiare
(to) say dire
school scuola (f.)
scooter motorino (m.)
screen schermo (m.)
sea mare (m.)
seat posto (m.)
(to) see vedere
(to) see again rivedere
second secondo
secret segreto
secretary segretario/a
(to) sell vendere
Senate Senato (m.)
senator senatore / senatrice
(to) send mandare
sense senso (m.)
September settembre (m.)
serious serio
(to) serve servire
set (service) servizio (m.)

(to) set up impostare
seven sette
seventeen diciassette
seventy settanta
several diversi (pl.)
(to) shake hands dare la mano
(to) shave radersi
sheet (of paper) foglio (m.)
shirt camicia (f.)
shoes scarpe (f. pl.)
shop negozio (m.)
shop assistant commesso/a
shopping spesa (f.), spese (f. pl.)
(to) show far vedere
show spettacolo (m.)
shower doccia (f.)
side dish contorno (m.)
silk seta (f.)
sincere sincero
(to) sing cantare
singer cantante (m. & f.)
single singolo
sir signore
sister sorella (f.)
(to) sit down sedersi
six sei
sixteen sedici
sixth sesto
sixty sessanta
size misura (f.)
(to) ski sciare
skis sci (m. pl.)
(to) sleep dormire
slippers pantofole (f. pl.)
slowly piano
small piccolo
smaller, smallest minore
(to) smoke fumare
so così
soccer calcio (m.)
socialist socialista (m. & f.)
soft drink bibita (f.)
some qualche, alcuni
something qualcosa
son figlio (m.)
sorry scusi, [mi] dispiace

soup minestra (f.)
Spain Spagna (f.)
(to) speak parlare
specialty specialità
specially specialmente
spectacles occhiali (m. pl.)
spectator spettatore / spettatrice
(to) spend spendere
spokesperson portavoce (m. & f.)
sprain strappo (m.)
square (public) piazza (f.)
stamp francobollo (m.)
station stazione (f.)
(to) stay rimanere, restare, stare
steak bistecca (f.)
still ancora
Stock Exchange Borsa (f.)
stomach stomaco (m.)
stop fermata (f.)
(to) stop fermarsi
story storia (f.)
straight diritto
strike (labour) sciopero (m.)
stripe riga (f.)
student studente / studentessa
studious studioso
(to) study studiare
stupid stupido
suburbs periferia (f.)
(to) succeed riuscire
sugar zucchero (m.)
suitcase valigia (f.)
summer estate (f.)
sun sole (m.)
(to) sunbathe esporsi al sole
Sunday domenica (f.)
supermarket supermercato (m.)
supper cena (f.)
(to) support (sport) fare il tifo per
supporter (fan) tifoso/a
sure certo, sicuro
sweater maglione (m.)
(to) swim nuotare
swimming pool piscina (f.)
system sistema (m.)

(to) take prendere
(to) take back portare di ritorno
tall alto
(to) taste assaggiare
taxi taxi (m.)
teacher insegnante (m. & f.)
telegram telegramma (m.)
telephone telefono (m.)
television televisione (f.)
temperature febbre (f.)
ten dieci
tenor tenore (m.)
tent tenda (f.)
terrace terrazzo (m.)
Thank goodness! Meno male!
thank you grazie
that che
that is (i.e.) cioè
that which ciò che, quello che
the il (m.), la (f.)
theater teatro (m.)
then allora, dunque, poi
there li
thesis tesi (f.)
thing cosa (f.)
things roba (f.)
(to) think credere, pensare
thirst sete (f.)
thirteen tredici
thirty trenta
this questo
thousand mille
three tre
Thursday giovedì (m.)
ticket biglietto (m.)
tie cravatta (f.)
time (general) tempo (m.)
time (occasion) volta (f.)
time (of the day) ora (f.)
timetable orario (m.)
tip mancia (m.)
tired stanco
(to get) tired stancarsi
to a
tobacconist's tabaccaio (m.)
today oggi

toe dito (m.)
together with insieme a
toilet gabinetto (m.)
tomato pomodoro (m.)
tomorrow domani
tonight stasera
too anche
too much, too troppo
top cima (f.)
tourist tax tassa di soggiorno (f.)
town città (f.)
trade union sindacato (m.)
traffic traffico (m.)
tragic tragico
train treno (m.)
transportation trasporto (m.)
(to) travel viaggiare
tricky delicato
trip gita (f.)
trout trota (f.)
true vero
truth verità (f.)
Tuesday martedì (m.)
twelve dodici
twenty venti
two due

ugly brutto
unbeatable insuperabile
uncle zio (m.)
under sotto
(to) understand capire, intendere
unfortunately purtroppo
uniform divisa (f.)
unique unico
university università (f.)
until finché … non, fino ... a
unwell indisposto
(to) use usare

vacuum cleaner aspirapolvere (m.)
valid valido
veal vitello (m.)
veal cutlet cotoletta (f.)
vegetable verdura (f.)
vegetarian vegetariano/a

Venice Venezia (f.)
very molto
very bad pessimo
very well benissimo
violinist violinista (m. & f.)
visit visita (f.)
(to) visit (a person) andare a trovare
(to) visit (a place) visitare
voice voce (f.)
vote voto (m.)
(to) vote votare
voucher buono (m.)

(to) wait aspettare, attendere
waiter / waitress cameriere/a
walk passeggiata, camminata (f.)
(to) walk camminare
(to) want volere
warm caldo
(to) warn avvisare
(to) wash lavare
  (to) wash oneself lavarsi
washing machine lavatrice (f.)
watchmaker orologiaio/a
water acqua (f.)
way senso (m.)
(to) wear portare
Wednesday mercoledì (m.)
week settimana (f.)
welcome benvenuto/a/e/i
west ovest (m.)
what che, che cosa
whatever qualsiasi, qualunque

when quando
where dove
where from di dove
which quale, che
white bianco
who? chi
who, whom che, il quale, cui
why perché, come mai
wife moglie (f.)
willingly volentieri
window finestra (f.)
winter inverno (m.)
wish voglia (f.)
(to) wish desiderare
with con
wood legno (m.)
world mondo (m.)
worried preoccupato
(to) worry preoccuparsi
worse peggiore
worse (adv.) peggio
(to) write scrivere
wrong sbagliato, torto

year anno
yes sì
yesterday ieri
yet ancora
you tu (fam.), Lei (formal), voi (pl.)
young giovane
younger, youngest minore

zero zero (m.)
zip(per) cerniera (f.)
zoo zoo (m.)

Index

The numbers refer to sections unless a page or a particular conversation in a week is specified.